ISLAM AND THE MUSLIM WORLD

No. 14

General Editor: JOHN RALPH WILLIS
Department of History, University of California, Berkeley

THE CALIPHS
AND THEIR NON-MUSLIM SUBJECTS

THE CALIPHS

AND THEIR

NON-MUSLIM SUBJECTS

A Critical Study of the Covenant of 'Umar

BY

A. S. TRITTON

FRANK CASS & CO. LTD.
1970

Published by
FRANK CASS AND COMPANY LIMITED
67 Great Russell Street, London WC1

First edition   1930
New impression   1970

ISBN 0 7146 1996 5

Printed in Great Britain by Clarke, Doble & Brendon Ltd.
Plymouth and London

INTRODUCTORY NOTE
TO THE
1970 REPRINT

SINCE this book was first published, more recent studies have shown that the earlier part of the chapter on taxation is too generalized and ignored local differences. Individual statements are correct but have not been properly co-ordinated. This does not however apply to the sections after page 215 and two books may be named to remedy the deficiences:— F. Lokkegaard, *Islamic Taxation*, (1950) and D. C. Dennett, *Conversion and the Po; tax in the early Islam* (1951)

A.S.T.

September 1969.

PREFACE

IN the middle of India it is hard to get books; I could find only one Jewish book and some only of the Christian authorities. This explains some of the deficiencies of my work. Much more than appears between inverted commas is translation, hence some variations in spelling and some unevenness in the English. My debt to von Kremer, Mez, Browne, Shedd, and Sir T. W. Arnold is obvious. Chapters VIII and XIII appeared in the *Journal of the Royal Asiatic Society*; the former has been rewritten and the latter revised. I used Mr. H. I. Bell's translation of the papyri. He suggests that the three taxes mentioned on p. 201 are land tax, poll-tax, and the tax for the support of officials. If some of the tales told by Muslims and repeated here are not true, it does not matter much. If invented, they must have been possible at the time of invention, or the inventor thought that they represented the true Muslim policy.

Dates are of the Hejira unless otherwise marked. The only contraction used is 'b.', 'son of'. Arabic history is full of proper names; only the more important are put in the index.

It is a pleasant duty to thank Prof. W. B. Stevenson, of Glasgow, Maulvi Abd ul Aziz Memon and Dr. S. Hadi Hasan, of Aligarh, for help given. The last named also undertook the wearisome task of reading the proofs.

A.S.T.

TABLE OF CONTENTS

INTRODUCTION

AFTER the death of Muhammad, in A.D. 632, his community was ruled by three caliphs, who kept Medina, the City of the Prophet, as their capital. That was the time of the most spectacular conquests. The system of administration was simple. Arabs were appointed governors of the provinces and to a few of the chief posts in them, while most of the subordinate officials retained their posts. The great innovation was that the Arabs became the standing army and militia, and were paid by the state to protect it, the provincials supplying the money. Such organization of the state as there was was the work of 'Umar I, who ruled from A.H. 13 to 23, A.D. 634 to 644.

From A.H. 40 to 132, A.D. 661 to 750, the Umayyad caliphs ruled. They moved the capital to Damascus, where the government was surrounded by a Christian population and exposed to the influence of an old civilization. Mu'āwia, the first caliph, owed his success largely to having done his duty as an Arab and avenged the murder of 'Uthmān, and in consonance with this he and his successors lived as Arab chiefs rather than as rulers of a great empire. They were Arabs first and Muslims second. The words attributed to Mu'āwia, 'I found that the people of Egypt were of three sorts, one-third men, one-third like men, and one-third not men, i.e. Arabs, converted foreigners, and those who pretend to be Muslims, the Copts', reveals the Umayyad mind.[1]

[1] M., 1, 50.

The words, ' those who pretend to be Muslims ', are probably an addition, but otherwise the saying may well be genuine. The chief distinction in that age was to be an Arab.

At first the idea was that no Muslim paid anything to the state, rather he was kept by it. In theory all revenue, except the profits of crown lands, came from non-Muslims. It is doubtful how far the religious taxes paid by Muslims were applied to their rightful object, the relief of the poor; they may have gone into the common purse of the state. As the provincials turned Muslim, and claimed exemption from tribute, the revenue diminished, and it was found necessary to compel the converts to pay. 'Umar II (A.H. 99–101, A.D. 717–720), who modelled himself on his namesake, tried to make a state in which all Muslims were equal, but died before he could accomplish much. Throughout the dynasty the antithesis was between Arab and non-Arab.

It was a popular saying at Damascus that under the caliph Walīd men talked of fine buildings, under Sulaimān of cookery and women, and under 'Umar II of religion. The epigram illustrates the fact that the Umayyad caliphs took little interest in religion, and that Muslim law began its development away from the court and government.

The Umayyads fell as a result of internal strife and of an attack from without, which promised to elevate the family of the Prophet to the throne.

From A.H. 132 to 656, A.D. 750 to 1258, the Abbasids reigned, though they did not always rule. As they had been raised to power by Persians who were devoted to the family of the Prophet, the

Abbasid caliphs were Muslims first and then monarchs in the style of the Great King. As Muslims they were exact in the performance of their religious duties, and often genuinely interested in religion. As most of their supporters were Persians, the Arabs lost their place of pride, and any Muslim, whatever his race, might hope for success at court.

As the antithesis between Arab and non-Arab disappeared, so that between Muslim and non-Muslim was sharpened. The salaries of the Arabs were stopped and all men paid taxes, though non-Muslims still paid their special poll-tax.

At the beginning of the dynasty the Abbasids ruled the whole Muslim world except Spain. In the reign of Māmūn (A.H. 198–218, A.D. 813–833) we find hereditary governors of provinces, and about A.H. 250, A.D. 864, Egypt became practically independent under Ahmad b. Tūlūn. Then separate kingdoms arose in the east, while the caliphs entrusted their fortunes to Turkish mercenaries, who often tyrannized over their so-called masters.

In A.H. 334, A.D. 946, the Dailamite family of Buwaih, who belonged to the *shi'a* sect, conquered Baghdad, and the caliphs became puppets in the hands of schismatics.

In A.H. 358, A.D. 959, the Fatimid caliphs, who also belonged to the *shi'a* sect, conquered Egypt, and later Syria, and held them for two and a half centuries.

In A.H. 431, A.D. 1040, the Seljuk Turks founded a kingdom, and in A.H. 447, A.D. 1055, they took Baghdad. The caliph kept up the form of sovereignty with his vizier and ministers, but all power was in the hands of the Turks. When their might decayed, in A.H. 552, A.D. 1156, the Muslim world split into a number of small states, of which Baghdad, the seat of the caliph, was by no means the most important. Most of these were wiped out by the Mongols when they sacked Baghdad in A.H. 656.

Long before this the laws fixing the status of the non-Muslim subjects had been made, some by lawyers, some by caliphs. The lawyers' laws seem to have been complete by A.H. 200, A.D. 815, while the laws of Mutawakkil (A.H. 232–247, A.D. 847–861) sufficed for later monarchs, who only put them in force again. It depended on the temper of the monarch or the political exigencies of the time whether they were enforced or not.

CHAPTER I

THE COVENANT OF 'UMAR

UNDER the rule of the caliphs those who did not confess the Muslim faith were under certain restrictions both in public and private life. This was the price they paid for the privilege of living under Muslim government. The only religions recognized as entitled to this privilege were the Christian, Jewish, Magian, Samaritan, and Sabian. Adherents of these were called 'the people of protection' (*ahlu dh-dhimmati*) or *dhimmis*. It was held that the words of the Koran (9, 27), 'Until they pay tribute out of hand, and they be humbled', justified these restrictions. A list of them is contained in the 'covenant of 'Umar I'. This is recorded in several forms. One is given in a letter from 'Umar, in which he quotes a letter from some Christians.

'When you came to us we asked of you safety for our lives, our families, our property, and the people of our religion on these conditions; to pay tribute out of hand and be humiliated; not to hinder any Muslim from stopping in our churches by night or day, to entertain him there three days and give him food there and open to him their doors; to beat the *nākūs*[1] only gently in them and not to raise our voices in them in chanting; not to shelter there, nor in any of our houses, a spy of your

---

[1] A board beaten with a stick or hammer, taking the place of bells in eastern churches. In Spain the word is used for bell.

enemies ; not to build a church, convent, hermitage,[1] or cell, nor repair those that are dilapidated, nor assemble in any that is in a Muslim quarter, nor in their presence ; not to display idolatry nor invite to it, nor show a cross on our churches, nor in any of the roads or markets of the Muslims ; not to learn the Koran nor teach it to our children ; not to prevent any of our relatives from turning Muslim if he wish it; to cut our hair in front; to tie the *zunnār* round our waists ; to keep to our religion ; not to resemble the Muslims in dress, appearance, saddles, the engraving on our seals (that we should engrave them in Arabic) ; not to use their *kunyas* ;[2] to honour and respect them, to stand up for them when we meet together; to guide them in their ways and goings ; not to make our houses higher (than theirs); not to keep weapons or swords, nor wear them in a town or on a journey in Muslim lands ; not to sell wine or display it ; not to light fires with our dead in a road where Muslims dwell, nor to raise our voices at their (? our) funerals, nor bring them near Muslims ; not to strike a Muslim ; not to keep slaves who have been the property of Muslims. We impose these terms on ourselves and our co-religionists ; he who rejects them has no protection.'[3]

Another form of the covenant is given in a letter to Abū 'Ubaida, the chief commander in Syria and apparently from Damascus.

' When thou camest into our land we asked of thee

---

[1] *Kallāya*, Syriac *Kellitha*. In other copies the word is corrupt. It may stand for *Kallāya* or *Kullaisa*, which is found in the Mustatraf. *Kullais* was the name of a church in Sanaa, and has become a common noun.

[2] The titles, ' father of ', ' son of ', ' mother of '. [3] I.A., 1, 178.

safety for our lives and the people of our religion, and we imposed these terms on ourselves; not to build in Damascus and its environs church, convent, chapel, monk's hermitage, not to repair what is dilapidated of our churches nor any of them that are in Muslim quarters; not to withhold our churches from Muslims stopping there by night or day; to open their doors to the traveller and wayfarer; not to shelter there nor in our houses a spy, not to hide one who is a traitor to the Muslims; to beat the *nākūs* only gently in our churches, not to display a cross on them, not to raise our voices in prayer or chanting in our churches, not to carry in procession a cross or our book, not to take out Easter or Palm Sunday processions; not to raise our voices over our dead, nor to show fires with them in the markets of the Muslims, nor bring our funerals near them; not to sell wine nor parade idolatry in companies of Muslims; not to entice a Muslim to our religion nor invite him to it; not to keep slaves who have been the property of Muslims;[1] not to prevent any relative from entering Islam if he wish it; to keep our religion wherever we are; not to resemble the Muslims in wearing the *kalansuwa*,[2] the turban, shoes, nor in the parting of the hair, nor in their way of riding; not to use their language nor be called by their names; to cut the hair in front and divide our forelocks; to tie the *zunnār* round our waists; not to engrave Arabic on our seals; not to ride on saddles; not to keep arms nor put them in our houses nor wear swords; to honour Muslims

---

[1] Ar-rakīku 'lladīna jarat 'alaihim sihām ul-muslimīn.   [2] A tall cap.

in their gatherings, to guide them on the road, to
stand up in public meetings when they wish it; not
to make our houses higher than theirs; not to
teach our children the Koran; not to be partners
with a Muslim except in business; to entertain
every Muslim traveller in our customary style and
feed him in it three days. We will not abuse a
Muslim, and he who strikes a Muslim has forfeited
his rights.'[1]

The version given in the *Mustaṭraf* is very like
Abū 'Ubaida's, but one phrase has been omitted
(whether by the fault of the compiler or a copyist
could only be decided by an examination of the
manuscripts), so that it reads, 'not to build in or
near our cities churches, convents, chapels, and
cells; not to repair those that are dilapidated by
day or night; to open their doors to the traveller
and wayfarer.'[2]

There are some very curious points in this
covenant. It is not usual for a conquered people to
decide the terms on which they shall be admitted to
alliance with the victors. Again, it is strange that
the conquered Christians should forbid themselves
all knowledge of the Koran, and yet quote it to the
caliph, 'to pay tribute out of hand and be humbled'.
The covenant is attributed now to 'Umar and now
to his general. This is not strange if it were
concluded by the general and ratified by the caliph.
It is strange that, in the popular form, it is a treaty
with a nameless town. If it had been made with
Damascus, the capital of the province, one would
expect the fact to have been remembered. The other

---

[1] I.A., 1, 149.   [2] Must., 1, 124.

alternative is that it was first made with a place
the name of which was forgotten, and then it was
assumed to be the treaty between Abū 'Ubaida and
Damascus. This view might be supported by the
existence of other treaties with Damascus. These
vary, from Khālid's—' This is what Khālid b. Walīd
gave to the inhabitants of Damascus. He gave them
security for their persons, property, churches, and
the wall of their city. None of their houses shall be
destroyed or confiscated. On these terms they have
alliance with God, and the protection of His Prophet,
the caliphs, and the believers. Nothing but good
shall befall them if they pay tribute,'[1] to such as
this—' These are the terms imposed on the *dhimmis*
of Syria (or Damascus); to bring back lost animals;
to build bridges for travellers out of their own means;
to entertain a Muslim traveller three days; not to
abuse or strike a Muslim; not to display a cross in
any gathering of Muslims; not to let a pig stray
into any Muslim house; not to carry wine in any
gathering of them; to light beacons for the soldiers;
not to betray the Muslims; not to build any new
church nor beat the *nākūs* before the call to prayer;
not to display flags in their feasts nor to carry arms
then; not to show arms in their houses.'[2]

On the other hand, no treaty with any Syrian
town at all resembles the covenant; they are all
quite simple. That with Hims may be taken as
typical. ' The inhabitants of Hims made peace with
him on condition that he gave them security for
their persons, property, the city wall, the churches
and the mills. He set apart a quarter of the church

[1] B., 121; I.A., 1, 241.   [2] I.A., 1, 150.

of St. John as a mosque, and imposed tribute on
those who remained.'[1] Even that with Jerusalem,
made by 'Umar in person, is not nearly so detailed.
The important clauses of it are. ' He gave them
security for their lives, property, churches, and
crosses, their sick and healthy, and the rest of their
religion. Their churches shall not be used as dwellings nor destroyed, nor they (the churches), nor
their estates, nor their crosses, nor their property be
diminished in any way. They shall not be persecuted for religion's sake. No Jew shall dwell with
them there. Whoso wishes to go to the Greeks
and take his property with him shall leave his
churches and crosses. There shall be no payment
of tribute till the harvest is gathered in.'[2]

Suspicion arises that the covenant is not the
work of 'Umar. It presupposes closer intercourse
between Christians and Muslims than was possible
in the early days of the conquest. We cannot save
it by arguing that it was legislation for the future.
That was not the way of 'Umar and his advisers;
as statesmen they lived from hand to mouth, and
did not look to the future. Sufficient proof of this
is found in the laws about tribute. These assumed
that the Arabs would continue to live on the labour
of the *dhimmis*; so that when these latter were converted in crowds to Islam, the finances of the state
and the state itself received a grievous and quite un-
expected shock. It has been argued that Syria was
the frontier province and more exposed to war with
Byzantium, therefore, it was needful to impose
special restrictions on the inhabitants. To which it

[1] B., 131.   [2] T., I, 2405.

is enough to say that only part of the province was exposed to the danger of foreign war, that al Jazīra —North Mesopotamia—was in the same or even a higher degree the seat of war with the Greeks, and we hear nothing of these rules being enforced there. Later they were more or less enforced throughout the Muslim world, but there is no evidence to show that they were enforced in Syria in the days of 'Umar.

But this is not all. There is another form of the covenant which is said to have been reached after a conversation between 'Umar, Abū 'Ubaida, and the patrician Constantine. It runs as follows: ' These are the terms imposed on the Christians. The rich are to pay forty-eight dirhams, the middle class twenty-four, and the poor twelve. They are not to build churches, not to lift up a cross in the presence of Muslims, and to beat the *nākūs* inside the churches only. They are to share their houses that the Muslims may dwell in them, otherwise I ['Umar] shall not be easy about you. They are to give that part of the churches towards Mecca as mosques for the Muslims, for they are in the middle of the towns. They are not to drive pigs into the presence of Muslims. They are to entertain them as guests three days and nights. They are to provide mounts, for those on foot, from village to village. They are to help them and not to betray them. They are not to make agreements with their enemies. He who breaks these conditions may be slain and his women and children made slaves.'[1]

---

[1] Ghazi, 389.

The conclusion forced on one is that no one knew what the covenant of 'Umar was; and that any collection of peace terms might be glorified with his name. It would seem that it was an exercise in the schools of law to draw up pattern treaties. One such is preserved in the *Kitāb ul Umm*. It may be quoted as the fullest statement of the limitations imposed on the people of the book. After a protocol, in which the name of the contracting country and its prince could be inserted, it proceeds:

' I, and all Muslims, promise you and your fellow Christians security as long as you and they keep the conditions we impose upon you. Which are: you shall be under Muslim laws and no other, and shall not refuse to do anything we demand of you. If any of you says of the Prophet, of God's book or His religion what is unfitting, he is debarred from the protection of God, the Commander of the Faithful, and all Muslims; the conditions on which security was given are annulled; and the Commander of the Faithful has put his property and life outside the pale of the law, like the property and lives of enemies. If one of you commits fornication with or marries a Muslim woman, or robs a Muslim on the highway, or turns a Muslim from his religion, or helps their enemies as a soldier or guide to Muslim weaknesses, or shelters their spies, he has broken his agreement, and his life and property are without the law. He who does lesser harm than this to the goods or honour of a Muslim shall be punished. We shall scrutinize your dealing with Muslims, and if you have done anything unlawful for a Muslim we shall undo it and punish you; e.g.

if you have sold to a Muslim any forbidden thing, as wine, pigs, blood, or an (unclean) carcase, we shall annul the sale, take the price from you (if you have received it) or withhold it from you (if it has not been paid); we shall pour out the wine or blood and burn the carcase. If he (the Muslim) wishes it to be destroyed we shall do nothing to him, but we shall punish you. You shall not give him any forbidden thing to eat or drink, and shall not give him a wife in the presence of your witnesses nor in an illegal marriage. We shall not scrutinize nor enquire into a contract between you and any other unbeliever. If either party wishes to annul the contract, and brings a request to us, if we think that it should be annulled we shall annul it, if it is legal we shall allow it. But if the object has been taken and lost we shall not restore it, for a sale between unbelievers has been finished. If you or any other unbeliever asks for judgment we shall give it according to Muslim law; if we are not approached we shall not interfere between you. If you kill accidentally a Muslim or an ally, Christian or not, then the relatives (of the homicide) shall pay blood money, as among Muslims. For you, relatives are on the father's side. If a homicide has no relatives then his estate must pay. A murderer shall be killed unless the heirs wish to take blood money, which shall be paid at once. A thief, if his victim complains, shall have his hand cut off, if this is the punishment, and shall pay a fine. The slanderer shall be punished if the punishment is fixed; if not, he shall be punished according to Muslim law. You shall not display in any Muslim town the cross nor parade your idolatry, nor build a church nor place of assembly for your prayers, nor beat the *nākūs*, nor use your idolatrous language about Jesus, the son of Mary, to any Muslim. You shall wear the *zunnār* above all your clothes, cloaks and others, so that it is not hidden; you shall use peculiar saddles and manner of riding, and make your *kalansuwas* different from those of the Muslims by a mark you put on them. You shall not take the crest of the road nor the chief seats in assemblies, when Muslims are present. Every free adult male of sound mind shall pay poll-tax, one dinar of full weight, at new year. He shall not leave his town till he has paid and shall not appoint a substitute to pay it, one who pays no *jizya* till the beginning of the year. A poor man is liable for his *jizya* till it is paid; poverty does not cancel any of your obligations nor abrogate the protection given you. [Text?] If you have anything we shall take it. The *jizya* is the only burden on your property as long as you stay in your town or travel in Muslim land, except as merchants. You may not enter Mecca under any conditions. If you travel with merchandise you must pay one-tenth to the Muslims, you may go where you like in Muslim land, except Mecca, and may stay in any Muslim land you like except the Hedjaz, where you may stay three days only till you depart.

‘ These terms are binding on him who has hair under his clothes, is adult, or has completed fifteen years before this date, if he agrees to them; if not, there is no treaty with him. Your little boys, immature lads, lunatics, and slaves do not pay *jizya*.

If a lunatic becomes sane, a boy grows up, a slave is set free and follows your religion, he pays *jizya*. The terms are binding on you and those who accept them; we have no treaty with those who refuse them. We will protect you and your lawful (according to our law) property against any one, Muslim or not, who tries to wrong you, as we protect ourselves and our own property; our decisions about it will be the same as those about our own property, and ourselves. Our protection does not extend to forbidden things, like blood, carcases, wine and pigs, but we will not interfere with them; only you must not obtrude them on Muslim towns. If a Muslim or other buys them we will not force him to pay, for they are forbidden and have no price; but we will not let him annoy you about them, and if he does it again we will punish him, but will not force him to pay. You must fulfil all the conditions we have imposed on you. You must not attack a Muslim nor help their enemies by word or deed.

' The treaty of God and His promise and the most complete fulfilment of promise He has imposed on any of His creatures; you have the treaty of God and His promise and the protection of N.N. the Commander of the Faithful, and of the Muslims to fulfil their obligations towards you. Your sons, when they grow up, have the same obligations as you. If you alter or change them then the protection of God, of N.N. the Commander of the Faithful, and of the Muslims is taken from you. He who is at a distance, yet receives this document and approves it, these are the terms that are binding on him and on us, if he approves them; if he does not approve, we have no treaty with him.'[1]

The object of the following chapters is to trace the rise of these various enactments, as far as that is possible. One difficulty is that most Muslim historians pay very little attention to the affairs of the *dhimmis*. Another is that in the east law is often the expression of the will or whim of the ruler. Laws are made and obeyed as long as the lawgiver is interested in them. When he grows bored with one subject or starts another hobby, things return in a short while to their old course. We shall see many examples of this.

Before going into details there is one general remark to be made. In theory the *dhimmi* had to fulfil all the conditions of the covenant if he would claim protection. In practice a few actions only put him outside the protection of Muslim law. The lawyers did not entirely agree what these actions were.

Mālik, Shāfe'i, and Ahmad b. Hanbal hold that failure to pay the poll-tax deprives them of protection. This was not the view of Abū Hanīfa. Ahmad and Mālik hold that four things put the *dhimmi* outside the law—blasphemy of God, of His book, of His religion, and of His Prophet.

Abū l Kāsim said that eight deeds made a *dhimmi* an outlaw. They are an agreement to fight the Muslims, fornication with a Muslim woman, an attempt to marry one, an attempt to pervert a Muslim from his religion, robbery of a Muslim on the highway, acting as a spy for unbelievers or sending

---

[1] Umm, 4, 118.

them information or acting as guide to them, and the killing of a Muslim man or woman.[1]

Abū Hanīfa taught that they must not be too severe with *dhimmis* who insulted the Prophet. Shāfe'i said that one who repented of having insulted the Prophet might be pardoned and restored to his privileges. Ibn Taimiya taught that the death penalty could not be evaded.[2]

---

[1] Mizan, 2, 162.   [2] Andrae, *Person Muhammeds*, 268.

CHAPTER II

GOVERNMENT SERVICE

WHEN the Arabs consolidated their conquests they took over the administrative system they found there and those officials who had not fled. An historical parallel is given by the action of Ibn Sa'ūd, the sultan of Nejd, when he conquered the Turkish province of Hufūf. None of his Arabs could or would do the clerical work of the minister of finance; it would not have been politic to employ a local merchant; so he kept the Turkish official in his service. Sometimes the Arabs were in straits to find suitable men. When the capture of Cæsarea put a finish to the conquest of Palestine the prisoners were sent to the caliph 'Umar. Some he gave as slaves to orphans of the Ansār: some he made clerks and employed in government service.[1] Abū Mūsā al Ash'ari had a Christian secretary.[2] On the other hand, it is reported that 'Umar refused to employ a Christian of Hīra.[3] It is said that Mu'āwia was jealous of 'Abd ur Rahmān b. Khālid, and bribed his physician, Ibn Uthāl, a Christian, to poison him. He rewarded the doctor by releasing him from the payment of tribute and making him collector of taxes in Hims.[4]

It was not till the reign of 'Abd ul Malik that official records began to be kept in Arabic instead

---

[1] B., 142.   [2] 'Uyun, 1, 43 ; Ghazi, 388.   [3] 'Uyun, 1, 43.
[4] T., II, 82 ; Agh., 15, 12. Wellhausen doubts the appointment at Hims.

of in Greek, Persian, and Coptic. As told by
Balādhuri, the story shows that the active head of
the finance department was a Syrian in Syria and
in Persia a Persian. Sarjūn, who had been appointed first by Mu'āwia, was secretary to the caliph and
said to his co-religionists, 'Seek your livelihood in
another profession, for God has taken this from you.'[1]
This gloomy prediction was not fulfilled; indeed
Sarjūn b. Mansūr was succeeded by his son, and
it was seldom that no Christians were to be found
in government service.[2] As late as 253 a receipt
for taxes in Egypt was written in both Arabic and
Greek.[3] In Isfahan Arabic was first used in the
government offices in the time of Abū Muslim.[4]
While Walīd b. 'Ukba was governor of Kūfa a
Christian was head of a prison near the town, c. 26.[5]

In Egypt the Byzantine officers were retained.
One, named Menas, who had been made prefect of
the north province by Heraclius, and who, being
presumptuous and illiterate, detested the Egyptians,
was kept at his post by the Muslims after the conquest. Another, Shenouti, was made governor of the
Rīf, and Philoxenus governor of Arcadia or Fayyūm.
These men loved the pagans, detested the Christians,
and forced them to bring to the Muslims forage,
milk, honey, fruit, raisins, and many other things
over and above the ordinary rations.[6] This Menas
squeezed 32,056 pieces of gold out of Alexandria as
tribute. He was replaced by John, who paid 22,000,
the rightful sum fixed by the treaty.[7]

Athanasius, a native of Edessa, who held office in

---

[1] B., 193, 300.   [2] M., 1, 98.   [3] Rainer, 787.   [4] I.R., 196.
[5] Agh., 4, 183.   [6] J.N., 375.   [7] J.N., 384.

Egypt, is comparatively well known. Marwān first appointed him along with Isaac, another Christian. He became head of the government offices in Alexandria, and led the other Christian officials in making a petition to the governor about church affairs. In official correspondence he is the 'glorious secretary', and in his establishment are twenty and again forty-four clerks. He was treasurer to 'Abd ul 'Azīz. Finally he was dismissed, and one Abū Yarbū' appointed in his place. On his return to Syria his property — all that he had acquired in Egypt — was confiscated. Legend has been busy with him. He is said to have been paid 60,000 dinars a year and one dinar from every soldier. Bar Hebræus says that his fame reached 'Abd ul Malik, who made him tutor to his little brother, 'Abd ul 'Azīz.[1] He grew very powerful, owned four thousand slaves, houses, villages, and gardens, and gold and silver like stones. From the rent of four hundred shops, which he owned in Edessa, he built the church of the Mother of God there. Sarjūn, who was a Melkite, envied him, and slandered him to the caliph, saying that he had stolen the treasures of Egypt. Moral suasion was employed, so Athanasius gave up what satisfied the caliph and still had much left for himself. In spite of exaggerations, it is clear that he had great power and used it for the benefit of his fellow Christians.

A certain Theodosius, who was a prominent Melkite, held a high position in Alexandria. He went to Yazīd, at Damascus, and, in return for a

---

[1] S., 116, 133, 135 ; B.M., 4 1447 ; K., 50, 59 ; M., 1, 98 ; B.H., 112 ; Lang., 247.

big sum of money, got a patent as governor of
Alexandria, Mareotis and their dependencies,
independent of the governor of Egypt. He was an
enemy of the Coptic patriarch, and used his position
to vex him. He extorted thirty-six dinars yearly as a
tax for his disciples (it is possible that at this time the
clergy, as such, did not pay taxes), the governor's
share of the requisitions for the fleet, besides other
monies.[1] There seems to be some exaggeration here,
but there is no reason to doubt that a Christian
could exercise great power.

During the patriarchate of Alexander (81–106)
Theodore was prefect of Alexandria.[2] In official
letters he is called Augustalis, which was the title in
Byzantine times of the prefect of Alexandria.[3] He
was probably the second in command under an Arab.
In the time of Hajjāj, Muhammad b. Marwān, the
governor of North Mesopotamia put to death
Anastasius b. Andrew, the headman of Edessa, and
the chronicler adds, ' up to that time Christians had
been secretaries, prefects, and governors of districts
for the Arabs.'[4]

'Umar II was shocked that non-Muslims should
exercise authority over Muslims, and tried to prevent it. His letter to the governors is instructive.
' To proceed ; God honoured, exalted and strengthened His people with Islam, and put humiliation
and shame on their opponents. He made them the
best nation that was created for men. We will not
give to their subjects authority over any one of them,
nor over their revenue ; lest they stretch out their
hands and tongues against them. We will humiliate

---

[1] S., 113, 137.   [2] S., 141.   [3] B.M., 4, 1392.   [4] S.A., 1, 294.

and disgrace them after that God had strengthened
and honoured them. We will expose them to
deceit and pride; and one is never safe from their
treachery. God says, "Take not your friends from
outside yourselves" (K. 3, 114). They will not fail
to corrupt you, they desire your suffering. So do
not choose Jews and Christians as friends.' In
Egypt he removed some of the Coptic officials and
replaced them by Muslims. Indeed, he claims to
have done this throughout the empire, for he writes,
' I do not know a secretary or official in any part of
your government who was not a Muslim but I dismissed him and appointed in his stead a Muslim.'[1]

The caliph Sulaimān made a Christian secretary,
al Batrīk b. Nakā, overseer of his constructions in
Ramla (Palestine), water channels, wells, and a
mosque.[2]

About this time Muslims are found in subordinate
government posts. The pay of an Arab clerk and
the upkeep of his horses is an item in the accounts
between A.D. 714 and 716.[3] In A.D. 710 an Arab, or
at least a Muslim, is postmaster in a small town.[4]
This is perhaps significant, for in later times the
postmaster was also in the secret service. Hishām,
in a letter to Khālid ul Kasri, refers to ' what you
have done in the way of asking help from Magians
and Christians, and making them rule over the necks
of the Muslims, and collecting their taxes, and exer-
cising authority over them.'[5] Mansūr appointed a
Jew, Mūsā, one of the two collectors of revenue.[6] It

---

[1] K., 60; Umar, 165; Ath., y. 101; S., 143.
[2] B., 143.   [3] B.M., 4, 1434.   [4] B.M., 4, 1347.
[5] Mubarrad, 790.   [6] Lang., 261; C.M., 248.

is clear that the relations of Christians with authority were sometimes very easy. Bukām, a rich man from Būra, in Egypt, came to Māmūn and asked to be made headman of his town. The caliph said, 'Turn Muslim, become my client, and I will make you headman.' Bukām replied, 'You have ten thousand Muslim clients and not one Christian.' Māmūn laughed, and made him headman of Būra and district.[1]

Mutawakkil re-enacted the law that no non-Muslim should be in government service ;[2] he even went so far as to dismiss, in 247, the Christian keeper of the Nilometer. Abū Raddād was appointed in his place at a salary of six, or, according to another story, seven dinars monthly.[3] At the accession of Muktadir, however, the Christian secretaries had become powerful again, so complaint was made to the caliph, and in 296 he dismissed them. 'But this did not last long.'[4] In 313 a Christian was secretary to the head of the *diwan* of Lower Mesopotamia, one was head of the *diwan* of the palace, and two more were heads of the private *diwan* and the treasury.[5] In 319, when Husain b. Kāsim was intriguing to become vizier, he thought it worth while to curry favour with the Christian secretaries.[6] Many of the prominent men of that time had Christian secretaries, Ibn abī Sāj, governor of Armenia and Adharbaijān, Muflih, the eunuch, 'Ali b. 'Isā, the vizier, Abū Sulaimān b. Daud b. Hamdān, one of the family ruling in Mosul, Munis the Victorious, and the sons of Rāik.[7] Ahmad b.

---

[1] Eut., 2, 434. [2] M., 2, 494. [3] K., 203, 507. [4] 'Arib., 30. [5] 'Arib., 125.
[6] 'Arib., 164.   [7] 'Arib., 31, 112, 135, 159, 169 ; Ecl., 1, 218.

Tūlūn employed a Christian architect, but lost his temper with him, beat him and threw him into prison. When he wanted to build a new mosque it was suggested that he should take pillars from churches in deserted villages and the Delta. He refused, because such pillars were unclean and he wished to build his mosque with clean money. His architect heard of the dilemma, and sent a message from prison that he could build a mosque without pillars except the two beside the *mihrāb*. Ahmad had him brought from prison, his uncut hair hanging over his face, and questioned him. He sketched the mosque on a piece of parchment, and was given the work. When it was finished he received a present of ten thousand dinars and a comfortable provision till his death.[1] The village of Andūna was named after a Christian servant of Ahmad, one whom he had dismissed and fined fifty thousand dinars.[2]

In Baghdad a Christian vizier, 'Abdūn b. Sā'id, visited the *kadi*, Ismail b. Ishāk, who rose up to greet him. He noticed that the witnesses and the rest of the company disapproved of his action. When the vizier had gone, he said, ' I noticed your disapproval, but God has said, " God does not forbid you to have dealings with those who have not fought with you for religion's sake nor driven you out of your homes " (K. 60, 8). This man manages the business of Muslims, he is the ambassador between us and the caliph. What I did was right. This speech convinced those who listened to it.[3] One account says that non-Muslims were dismissed from government service by 'Amr b. l 'As, the caliphs 'Abd ul Malik and Māmūn, and the vizier Yahya b. Fadl.[1]

Ibn Saghā, who was named Paul, the Coptic secretary, was finance minister in Egypt during the Ikshhīd dynasty.[2] The Fatimids attached great importance to the post of chief secretary, and chose their secretaries, both Muslims and *dhimmis*, for their skill in writing. A poet said of the Jews under the Fatimids:

> The Jews of this age have attained their highest hopes and grown strong.
> Power is theirs and wealth, from them is chosen the counsellor and the king.
> Men of Egypt, turn Jews, I advise you ; the sky has turned Jew.[3]

It is stated definitely that in Spain and Morocco no Christians and no Jews were secretaries.[4]

Mukaddasi reports in the fourth century that the clerks in Syria and Egypt were Christians, as were most of the doctors in Syria.[5] In 369 the vizier in Baghdad was a Christian, Nasr b. Hārūn.[6] When Ibn ul Furāt was blamed for setting a Christian in command of the army, he defended himself against the charge of impiety by pleading the example of previous caliphs who had given office to Christians.[7] These Christian officers received all the usual marks of honour, for the Muslims objected to kissing their hands. In 387 two Christians were masters of the town of Dakūk, acted as rulers in it, and made the Muslims their servants. Some of these came to Jibrail b. Muhammad and said, ' You

---

[1] Ghazi, 392 f.   [2] M., 1, 73.   [3] Husn, 2, 129, 146.
[4] Mak., 1, 134.   [5] Muk., 183.   [6] Ecl., 2, 406.   [7] Viziers, 95.

want to fight the unbelievers, here are two all ready for you.' He captured the two men and seized their property.[1] In 380 al 'Azīz, the caliph of Egypt, made 'Isā b. Nestorius vizier, and Manasseh, a Jew, his deputy in Syria. The vizier favoured the Christians and the deputy the Jews. Complaint was made, so the caliph tortured both of them, seized 300,000 dinars from 'Isā and a large sum from Manasseh.[2] Reference is made elsewhere to Abū Nasr, the Christian official in Baghdad.[3]

In 393 'Isā b. Nestorius and Fahd b. Ibrāhīm were in the service of al Hākim; in 400 Mansūr b. 'Abdūn was his chief minister, and in 401 Zar'a b. 'Isā.[4]

Abū Sa'd Ibrāhīm and Abū Nasr Hārūn were the sons of a Jew, Sahl of Tustar. One was a merchant and the other a banker, who also dealt in goods from Irak. They were famous for their extensive trade, and for giving back to the heirs things deposited with them by traders who had since died. For this they had a good reputation. They became important men. Ibrāhīm served the caliph az Zāhir, bought all manner of goods for him, and advanced in favour. Az Zāhir bought a black slave girl from him, was pleased with her, and begat Mustansir on her. She furthered the interests of Ibrāhīm, and when Mustansir became caliph she advanced him and attached him to her own service. When al Jarjarāi died, Ibn ul Anbāri became vizier. Abū Nasr went to pay his respects to the new vizier, and one of the servants insulted him. He expected

---

[1] Ath., y. 387; B.H., 201. [2] Ath., y. 380 ; Iyas, 1, 48.
[3] B.H., 205. [4] M., 2, 286.

the vizier to rebuke the man and apologise, but the opposite happened, and he was again insulted. He then complained to his brother, who at once set the queen-mother against the vizier. She persuaded her son to dismiss him and appoint Abū Nasr Sadaka b. Yūsuf in his place. He was a creature of Ibrāhīm, and did as he was told. This was in 436. Though not a minister, Ibrāhīm was the power behind the throne.[1]

In Persia the minister of Malikshah, Nizām ul Mulk, was alarmed at the employment of *dhimmis* by the government in place of Turks. In 484 he wrote : ' If a Jew or Christian, Magian or Karmathian, gets a position of authority or does the work of a Turk, carelessness is their chief characteristic ; there is no respect for religion, no love for the state, and no pity for the subjects. They (Jews, etc.) become very rich. The author fears the evil eye and knows not how this may go. In the days of Mahmūd, Mas'ūd, Tughril, and Alp Arslān no Magian, Jew, Christian, or heretic had the boldness to take part in public life.'[2] Probably the writer was the victim of a common weakness, and ascribed to the past a virtue it did not possess.

In 501 Majd ud Dīn b. Muttalib was made vizier of the caliph in Baghdad, on condition that he did not employ any *dhimmis* in the government offices.[3] In 506 a Jew, Abū Minjā b. Isaiah, was the engineer or surveyor in charge of digging the canal called by his name.[4] In 519 al Amir did without a vizier, and appointed two heads for the government offices, one of whom was a Samaritan, Abū Ya'kūb Ibrāhīm, and

---

[1] M., 1, 424. [2] Siyasetnameh, 139. [3] Ath., y. 501. [4] M., 1, 72.

a private secretary, Ibn abī Najāh, a monk. This last lorded it over the people, directed the ministry, and extorted money from the Christians. Then he began to squeeze everybody — officials, tax-farmers, and others—till all, headmen, *kadis*, and clerks, suffered from his exactions. Then al Amir had him put to death.[1] In 529 al Hāfiz made Tāj ud Dawla Bahrām, an Armenian Christian, his vizier. He dismissed Muslims and appointed Armenians, and generally oppressed the Muslim population. Ridwān led a riot against him, so he fled to Aswān, and was killed there in 531.[2] Asad ud Dīn Shirkuh, the conqueror of Egypt, had joined Nūr ud Dīn because he had killed a Christian secretary in Tekrit.[3] In Egypt he probably obeyed the orders of Nūr ud Dīn, and dismissed all Christians from the civil service, though Saladin certainly employed them. Nūr ud Dīn dismissed all Christians from public service in Mosul, and all employed in the palace, except 'Abdūn, his servant, an old, prudent man, rich in gold and knowledge.[4] In 569, when the Egyptians were conspiring with the Franks against Saladin, he used a Christian to discover their secrets.[5]

The manner of collecting the taxes in Egypt and an irregularity in the same are described by Makrīzi. When the Nile fell and sowing began, headquarters sent out a prudent man with reliable assessors who knew about the tribute, and often a Christian clerk, to survey the crops, etc ; then in the fourth Coptic month valiant soldiers, reliable clerks, and a different Christian clerk, to receive one-third of the tribute.[6]

[1] M., 2, 291. [2] Ath., y. 531. [3] B.H. Mu., 370.
[4] S.A., 2, 168. [5] Ath., y. 569. [6] M., 1, 86.

In the reign of al Hāfiz lidīn illah, when the Nile flood was over, witnesses, Christians, and clerks were sent to the provinces to measure the irrigated and cultivated land and to record the taxes. The collector, surveyor and witnesses went to measure a district. A Christian clerk had stayed behind, and wished to cross the river into the district to catch up with them. A boatman took him across and asked for payment. The clerk was angry, cursed him, and said, 'I am the surveyor, and you want me to pay the fare for crossing!' The boatman said, 'If I have a field, take it;' seized his mule's bridle and threw it into the boat. So the Christian had to pay the fare. When the survey was finished, and he made a clean copy of the assessment to take to the office in the capital, as was customary, he added twenty feddans to the total, and left a blank on one page. He showed the list to the witnesses and got their signatures to its accuracy. Then he wrote in the blank: 'The field of the Bridle, the name of the boatman, twenty feddans, a fief, four dinars the feddan, total eighty dinars'; and took the assessment to the ministry of finance. It was the custom, when four months of the financial year had elapsed, to send dare-devil soldiers, clerks, witnesses, and a Christian clerk to the provinces to collect one-third of land tax according to the assessment. This was spent on the army, which then had no estates as it has now. It was usual not to send the man who made the survey, but others. When the collector, the clerk, and the witnesses went to collect one-third of the revenue, they summoned the farmers on the basis of the assessment, among them the boatman, and they forced him to pay twenty-six and two-thirds dinars, one third of the eighty in the list. He denied having any land in the district, and the villagers supported him. The collector, a hard man, refused to listen, beat him with a whip, appealed to the signatures of the witnesses on the assessment, and made him sell his boat and what not to pay the third of the tax.

The boatman went to Cairo and told his story to the caliph. The tax lists were examined, and no mention of the field of the Bridle was found in them. The guilty clerk was paraded round the various offices, and all Christians were dismissed from government service. Now al Hāfiz believed in astrology, so the Christian clerks bribed his favourite astrologer to tell him that Egypt would flourish if a certain Christian were given power in the land. The caliph fell into the trap, and made this man, al Akhram b. Zakariah, head of the offices. He at once appointed more Christians than ever. They showed off their wealth by wearing fine clothes, and riding horses of the best breed. They oppressed the Muslims, seized the property of religious institutions, and kept Muslim slaves and slave girls. They even forced one Muslim clerk to sell his children to pay a fine.[1]

During the intrigues between the Egyptians and the Franks to drive Saladin out of Egypt, a Jewish secretary wrote the letters from Egypt.[2]

A Christian held some post in the army. He turned monk, and lived in the desert of the mountains of Hulwān. It is said that he discovered a treasure

---

[1] M., 1, 405. [2] M., 2, 22.

that had belonged to the caliph, al Hākim. With it he helped the poor and fugitive of every religion. His fame spread, and in three years he spent large sums. He was brought before the sultan, who treated him kindly, but he refused to reveal his secret. The sultan then threatened him and abused him, and, when his patience was exhausted, he tortured him till he died. Several legal opinions had been given that he ought to be put to death, lest he should lead weak Muslims astray. This happened in 666.[1] When Mansūr died, in 755, and Khalīl came to the throne, Christian clerks who were in the service of the emirs of the court became highminded towards the Muslims, wore gorgeous raiment and lived in great state. One was in the service of an emir named 'Ain ul Ghazāl. One day he met a broker who managed his chief's affairs. The broker dismounted and kissed the foot of the clerk, who began to curse and threaten him for his slowness in paying the price of some crops. The man excused himself humbly, but this only made the clerk behave more harshly. He told his servant to dismount, bind the broker, and lead him away. A crowd gathered, and accompanied him to the square before the mosque of Ibn Tūlūn. Many entreated him to release the man, but he refused. The crowd grew larger, threw him from his donkey, and set the broker free. He was then near his chief's house, who sent an officer with servants and soldiers to rescue him. They delivered him, and began to arrest some of the crowd to punish them. These raised a tumult, hurried to the castle, and implored the help

---

[1] Husn, 2, 176.

of Nasr ullah, the sultan. He sent to enquire into the matter, so they told him of the high-handed conduct of the Christian clerk towards the broker, and what had happened to themselves. He sent for 'Ain ul Ghazāl, and told the crowd to fetch the Christians to his presence. He also sent Badr ud Dīn Baidar and Sinjar, and bade them bring all the Christians before him to be killed. They appealed to him, and persuaded him to proclaim, in Old and New Cairo, that no Christian or Jew should serve the emirs. He bade the emirs propose to their Christian clerks to accept Islam; if they refused, they were to have their heads cut off; if they accepted, they might stop in their service. The same offer was made to all employees in the government offices. Many of the Christians hid themselves, and the mob burst into and plundered their houses; their women were made slaves and many were killed. Badr ud Dīn Baidar at last persuaded the sultan to send the governor of Cairo to make a proclamation that anyone plundering the house of a Christian would be hanged. Some were caught, paraded, and beaten. Many clerks of the sultan and emirs were collected, and made to stand a little distance from the sultan. He ordered some to be taken to the horse market, a great pit to be dug, the men to be thrown into it, and a fire lighted on top. Baidar interceded for them, but the sultan would not listen, saying, ' I will not have a Christian civil service in my kingdom.' Baidar obtained the grace that those who turned Muslim might remain in their service, while those who refused were to be beheaded. He took them to the palace of the deputy and said, ' My influence

availed with the sultan on one condition only.
Those who choose their own faith will be put to
death, those who choose Islam will be decorated and
remain in the service.' Then Makīn, one of the
chief secretaries, came forward and said, 'Sir, which
of our leaders will choose death for such a foul
faith? A faith for which we are killed and die, goes;
God has not set safety in it. Tell us which to
choose that we may go to it.' Baidar burst out
laughing and said, 'Shall we choose any but Islam?'
Makīn answered, 'We do not know, tell us and we
will obey you.' He then called the witnesses, and
recorded their conversion to Islam.[1]

A Christian secretary rode by the mosque of al
Azhar wearing boots and spurs, with an Alexandrian
jacket thrown over his head, runners in front to
save him from the pressure of the crowd, and
servants behind in fine clothes on light baggage
horses. This annoyed some Muslims, who sprang
at him, dragged him from his horse, and thought to
kill him. A crowd collected and they let him go.
Some of them spoke to the emir, Tāz, and he promised to get justice done them. They preferred a
complaint to the sultan, Sālih, in the presence of the
emirs, *kadis* and other dignitaries, asking for a
solemn court, to remind the Christians of the terms
imposed on them. The patriarch and the leading
Christians, with the head of the Jews and their
notables, were summoned to the sultan's presence.
The *kadi* 'Alā ud Dīn 'Ali, the private secretary,
read the covenant between the Muslims and the
protected, which they had brought with them. He

[1] M., 2, 497.

demanded from those present the acceptance of these terms, he recounted their many and repeated violations of the covenant, and they promised not to take service in the offices of the government or of the emirs, even though they pretended to be Muslims. They were, however, not to be forced to turn Muslim. Letters to this effect were sent to the local governors.

The mob pursued and attacked them, caught them in the streets, tore off their clothes and beat them; they did not leave them till they had turned Muslim. They lit fires to throw them in, so they hid in their houses and did not dare to show themselves abroad. The crowd followed up their weak points, and destroyed any houses that were higher than the Muslims'. The Christians were in sore straits, and neither they nor the Jews were seen in the streets. Complaint was made about the building of new churches, and several were pulled down. The governor of Cairo tried to restrain the mob, but it was too strong and the leaders were powerless to hold it.

Orders were published that no Jew or Christian was to be in government service, even though he had turned Muslim, for he would still associate with his Christian family. If anyone turned Muslim he was to be watched, to make sure that he observed the five daily prayers and those on Friday. When a Christian died Muslims were to be his executors, and if he had no heirs the treasury took his estate.[1]

Ambassadors. Christians were sometimes employ-

[1] M., 2, 499.

ed as envoys, especially to Christian powers. The patriarch, Dionysius, went to Egypt in 216, and, on his arrival, was sent by Māmūn to some rebels, to bring them back to their allegiance.[1]

When the musician, Ziryāb, went to Spain, Mansūr, a Jewish singer, was sent to meet him.[2]

About 344 the Spanish caliph, 'Abd ur Rahmān, received an embassy from king Otto, and sent back with them the bishop, Rabī'.[3] In the reign of Hakam II the chiefs of the protected Christians accompanied an ambassador.[4]

In 381 Lulu, the chamberlain of Sa'd ud Dawla, sent Malkūtha, the Syrian, to ask help from the emperor Basil.[5] The catholicus of Jerusalem and the patriarch of Antioch were forced to use their influence with the emperor to secure good treatment for Muslim captives.[6] Jamāl ud Dīn, vizier of Kutb ud Dīn, the emir of Mosul, sent Ignatius, the maphrian, as ambassador to George, king of Georgia, to ransom Arab captives. This happened about the year 560.[7]

ADDITIONAL NOTE

Many *dhimmis* became government officials and then accepted Islam; this happened so often that there is no need to give examples. Occasionally conversions were forced. Thus al Asbagh, son of 'Abd ul 'Azīz, the governor of Egypt, forced Butrus, an important official in upper Egypt, to be converted.[8] Persuasion was also used. Hafs, another governor of Egypt, announced that all *dhimmis* who abandoned

---

[1] S.A., 2, 266 f.   [2] Mak., 2, 85.   [3] Mak., 1, 235.   [4] Mak., 1, 249.
[5] Ecl., 3, 218, 220.   [6] Nish., 31.   [7] B.H., 328.   [8] S., 134.

their religion would be free from *kharāj*, which is *jizya*.[1]

In 755 many conversions took place in Egypt, in Kalyūb alone 450 in one day. The people turned Muslim and learnt the Koran. These conversions, however, were not altogether approved, for it was felt that they were only deceit and trickery, so that men might get posts under government and marry Muslim women. They succeeded so well that the race became quite mixed, and their descendants are in the majority.[2]

[1] S., 164 f.   [2] M., 2, 500.

CHAPTER III

CHURCHES AND MONASTERIES

In the covenant of 'Umar it was stipulated that Christians should neither build new churches nor repair ruinous ones and those situated in parts of towns inhabited by Muslims. This is an advance on the position in the time of Hārūn Rashīd, when a lawyer held that the terms were, 'that their churches should not be destroyed, neither within nor without the towns, but that they should not build new'.[1] He upheld his opinion by this statement, 'Any newly built church or chapel may be pulled down. Several caliphs wished to pull down churches, but the townsmen produced their charters and canon lawyers did not support the caliph's plans; for 'Umar's covenant stands till the day of resurrection'.[2] From this it is clear that churches had been built, and it is probable that the 'covenant of 'Umar' is not that known to us. There is an opinion, which may be old as it is attributed to Ibn 'Abbās: 'In a town which the Arabs founded Christians may not build a church nor beat the nākūs, . . . but in one founded by foreigners, and captured by Arabs, where they surrendered, they may do these things.'[3] This does not exhaust the variety of legal opinion; the views of the four schools are summarized in the following extract:

[1] Kh., 82.　　　[2] Kh., 87.　　　[3] Kh., 88.

' All schools agree that it is not allowed to build new churches or synagogues in towns or cities of Islam. They differ whether this is permitted in the neighbourhood (of towns). Mālik, Shāfe'i, and Ahmad do not permit it; Abū Hanīfa says that if the place is a mile or less from a town, it is not permitted; if the distance is greater, it is. Another question is, whether it is allowed to restore ruinous or rebuild ruined churches or synagogues in Islamic countries. Abū Hanīfa, Mālik, and Shāfe'i permit it. Abū Hanīfa adds the condition that the church is in a place that surrendered peaceably; if it was conquered by force, it is not allowed. Ahmad, according to the most probable version, which is also supported by some of his followers, and by famous Shāfe'ites like Abū Sa'īd al Istakhri and Abū 'Ali b. abī Huraira, says that the restoration of the ruinous and the rebuilding of the ruined is never permitted. Another version of his teaching is that restoration of the ruinous is allowed, but not rebuilding of the ruined. A third version allows both.'[1]

Bar Hebræus says that the Nestorian patriarch made an agreement with the Arabs, one of the terms of which was that the Arabs would help them to repair their old churches.[2]

The treaties with the various towns do not altogether support the legal view. Most guarantee the conquered the peaceful possession of their places of worship.[3] Those with towns in Persia usually guarantee the exercise of the *milla*, i.e. religious rites, and this must include the possession

---

[1] Mizan, 2, 211.   [2] B.H. Eccl., 2, 115 f.
[3] B., 130, 133, 147 ; T., I, 2655, 2657.

of the place of worship. In both Hims[1] and Hīt[2] the Muslims seized a quarter of a church. In Tiberias one treaty says that half the churches were taken by the Muslims, another left them all to their owners.[3] Three treaties with Edessa are quoted; two say nothing about religion, the third says that no new churches are to be built.[4] According to John of Nikiou, the Muslims in Egypt agreed not to seize any churches and not to interfere in any way with the Christians. In another place he adds, that 'Amr exacted the taxes which had been fixed, but took none of the property of the churches and committed no act of spoliation or plunder; nay, he preserved the churches to the end of his days.[5] In the treaty with Jerusalem it is said that 'Umar 'gave them protection for their lives, property, churches, and crosses, their sick and sound, and the rest of their religion. Their churches shall not be used as dwellings, nor destroyed, nor they (the churches) nor their estates, nor their crosses, nor their property be diminished in any way'. That with Lydda is almost identical.[6]

The story of the churches of Damascus is as complicated as that of its capture. Tabari says nothing about them. There are several forms of the treaty which Khālid is said to have made with them, and all guarantee the safety of the churches. The longest is this, ' He gave them security for their persons, property, churches, and the wall of their city. None of their houses shall be destroyed or dwelt in. For this they have the promise of God, and the protec-

[1] B., 131; Muk., 156; I.H., 117.   [2] B., 179.   [3] B., 116; Yak., 2, 159.
[4] B., 172, 174.   [5] J.N., 383.   [6] T., I, 2405 f.

tion of His Prophet, the caliphs, and the believers. Nothing but good shall befall them if they pay tribute.'[1] But Abū 'Ubaida is said to have seized half the churches, and a treaty in this sense and his name is recorded.[2] This is supported by the story of an appeal to 'Umar II. Hassān b. Mālik began a process against the natives of Damascus before 'Umar II about a church which a former governor had granted to him. 'Umar said, ' If it is one of the fifteen churches named in their treaty you have no case.'[3] Ibn 'Asākir also refers to these fifteen. He explains the Muslim possession of some churches on the ground that twelve patricians who had private chapels in their houses fled from the town, and the Muslims took the vacant dwellings. There is no reason to doubt the report that the natives of Damascus pleaded against the Arabs before 'Umar II about a church which someone—Ibn 'Asākir says Mu'āwia—had granted to the Banu Nasr in the city. 'Umar took it from them and gave it back to the Christians. Yazīd b. 'Abd ul Malik restored it to the Banu Nasr.[4]

It is now generally agreed that the tale of the division of the church of S. John between the Muslims and Christians is a myth. It is only the later historians who say that it was divided. It is curious that the Muslims are said to have taken the east end of the church and made a mosque of it. Now the altar stood at the east end, and the Christians would have made the most strenuous efforts to save that, the most sacred part of the church, for their own use and

[1] B., 121.   [2] I.A., 1, 178   [3] B., 124.   [4] B., 126 ; I.A., 1, 240.

worship. Further, the east end of the town is still the Christian quarter, so probably they always lived there, near their place of worship. Both Mu-'āwia and 'Abd ul Malik wished to take the whole church from the Christians, but they refused to surrender it. Walīd made the same attempt. He tried to buy it. When that failed he threatened to pull down the other churches in the town and district. According to another story, he threatened to seize the church of S. Thomas, which was some distance from S. John, for the latter is described as ' within '. Finally he had his way, and destroyed the church of S. John to enlarge the mosque. All accounts emphasize the fact that he destroyed the church. Abu 1 Fidā states that he destroyed a church which was beside the mosque, and incorporated it, i.e. the site, in the mosque. Balādhuri and Tabari say nothing of half a church   A pilgrim from the west, Arculphus, who visited Damascus in the reign of Mu'āwia, says distinctly, ' In which town the king of the Saracens has set up his rule and reigns, and a great church in honour of S. John the Baptist is established. In the same city has been made a church of the unbelieving Saracens, where they worship.' Everything shows that it was not till the reign of Walīd that the Muslims took possession of the church of S. John. To continue the story, when 'Umar II came to the throne, the Christians complained of Walīd's action. The caliph ordered the governor of Damascus to give the church back to them. The population of Damascus objected, ' Shall a mosque where we have prayed be turned into a church?' Finally it was agreed that the Christians should get the churches in the Ghuta, and give up all claim to S. John.[1] As a possible explanation of the problem of the other churches, one may suggest that the Muslims seized those in districts deserted by Christians, and the private chapels in deserted houses.

Most of the treaties do not agree with the regulations in the covenant. The conclusion, therefore, is that the authors of them knew nothing of it. If, as is highly probable, many of the treaties were composed by historians, an early date for the covenant is even less probable. The preceding paragraphs have given the theories of lawyers and historians. Historians and geographers often give details which show that the practice of rulers and subjects was not always according to law.

'Amr b. l 'As gave to the Makaukas part of the Lake of Habash as a burial ground for Christians.[2] In 60 or 61 part of the great church in Edessa was thrown down by an earthquake. Mu'āwia ordered it to be rebuilt.[3]

The church in the monastery of Beth 'Abhe was built about 25; perhaps before Muslim rule was established.[4] That of Mark in Alexandria was built between 39 and 56, though Severus puts it rather later.[5] The first church in Fustāt was built in Hārat ur Rūm while Maslama b. Mukhallad was governor, between 47 and 68.[6] When 'Abd ul 'Azīz founded Hulwān he allowed two Melkite servants of his to build a church there, and the patriarch built one also,

---

[1] I.A., 1, 199 ; B., 125 ; Abu l Fida, y. 96.
[2] M., 1, 124 ; Husn, 1, 68.   [3] S.A., 1, 288 ; C.M., 231.
[4] Thomas, 1, xliii.   [5] M., 2, 492 ; S., 119.   [6] A.S., 86.

because he had to pay his respects to the governor there. 'Abd ul 'Azīz told some bishops to build two convents there, and he allowed Athanasius, his secretary, to build a church in Kasr ush Shama'. He built two, Jurjis and Abū Kīr, within the castle and also one in Edessa.[1] Walīd took a copper gilt dome from the church in Baalbek and set it over the Rock in Jerusalem, and removed some marble pillars from the Church of Mary at Antioch for the mosque in Damascus. He destroyed a church, as the beating of the *nākūs* annoyed him.[2] 'Umar II is said to have commanded his governors not to destroy existing churches, but not to suffer the building of new.[3] Yazīd II ordered the destruction of churches, but died before it could be done.[4] In 104 Usāma b. Zaid, the surveyor of taxes in Egypt, attacked convents and destroyed churches. The caliph Hishām told him to let the Christians alone, according to their treaty.[5] The patriarch Kosmas went to Hishām, and by the help of some learned men was granted the Melkite churches in Egypt, which the Jacobites had seized. Hishām wrote to the governor to take these churches and give them to Kosmas.[6] Hishām wanted to build a mosque in Ramleh, and was told that the Christians had some marble pillars hidden in the sand ready for building a church. He told them to hand over those pillars, threatening to pull down the church at Lydda and use the columns from it for his mosque. The pillars were produced.[7]

Further east also the subject peoples were treated

[1] A.S., 157 ; Eut., 2, 369 f. ; Lang., 247.
[2] Eut., 2, 372 ; Mas., 3, 408 ; 5, 381.   [3] T., II, 1371 f.   [4] S., 144.
[5] M., 2, 492 f.   [6] Eut., 2, 386.   [7] Muk., 165.

equally generously. In the treaty with Adherbaijān the Arabs agreed not to kill or take prisoner anyone, not to destroy any fire temple, not to oppress the Kurds, especially not to prevent the people of Shīz from dancing at their feasts and doing in public what they were wont to do.[1] In the fourth century there were still so many fire temples ' that it would be impossible to know them without a list'. In every district were many, and one is said to have cost thirty million dirhams.[2] That temple in the town of Akhurīn was very holy, and people visited it from all parts of the country.[3] That in Medain is said to have an income bigger than the tribute of the province of Fars.[4] Kermān remained Magian throughout the time of the Umayyads, and turned Muslim only under the Abbasids.[5] When the town of Rūr surrendered it was stipulated that the idol was not to be injured. The Arab commander said that the idol was in the same position as the churches of the Christians and the fire temples of the Magians.[6] The general's opinion became so common that Abū Yūsuf, writing during the reign of Rashīd, elevates it into a principle, and says that tribute was taken from polytheists. But Māmūn did not recognize it when he compelled the pagans of Harrān to choose between Islam and death.[7] When Afshīn was brought to trial he was faced with two men whom he had flogged. He defended himself in these words: ' I inflicted on each of them a thousand stripes because I had covenanted with the princes of Sughd that I would leave all men unmolested in the religion which

[1] B., 236. [2] I.H., 189. [3] I.R., 165. [4] I.R., 186. [5] I.H., 221.
[6] B., 439. [7] Kh., 75 ; Fih., 320.

they professed, and these two fell upon a temple wherein were idols worshipped by the people of Ushrūsna, cast them forth, and made the place into a mosque. Wherefor I punished each of them with a thousand stripes, because they had acted aggressively and hindered the people in their worship.'[1]

The Arabs did not always take their treaty obligations seriously. Abdulla b. Kulaib is celebrated as the first man who struck his sword on the gate of Constantinople and gave the call to prayer in the empire. The emperor made known his desire to have him killed. Abdulla said, ' If you kill me, not a church will be left in the lands of Islam undestroyed.'[2] This may have been an empty boast.

It was not unknown that Muslims and Christians met on peaceful terms in a church. Mas'ūdi relates that he discussed the Trinity with a Christian, named Abū Zakaria, in the Green Church at Baghdad.[3] It was forbidden to whitewash fire temples lest they should look like mosques.[4]

During the conquest of Spain the Muslims were much less tolerant. On one of his expeditions Mūsā destroyed every church and broke every bell.[5] When Marida surrendered the Muslims took the property of those killed in the ambush, of those who fled to Galicia, of the churches, and the church jewels.[6]

Khālid ul Kasri (after 105) built a church for his mother behind the south-west wall of the mosque in Kūfa. They beat the *nākūs* when the call to prayer was given, and their loud chanting drowned the

[1] T., III, 1309.   [2] I.R., 193.   [3] Mas.T., 155.   [4] Ghazi, 394.
[5] Mak., 1, 174.   [6] Mak., 1, 171.

voice of the imām.[1] About this time, or rather earlier, Damisius, of Asfant, in Egypt, built a great monastery in the mountains.[2] About 117 Walīd b. Rifā'a, the governor of Egypt, allowed the church of Abū Mīna, in Hamrā, to be built (restored). ' This was after the conflict with the Arabs, when the Christians complained to the governor that their women and children were not safe from molestation while going to and returning from churches in Misr, especially on the nights of the forty days fast. In consequence of these outrages, a great number of the Arabs were killed.' Many Muslims complained of the building of this church; one account makes it produce an Arab riot.[3]

About 125 'Ishoyahbh, the abbot of Beth 'Abhe, pulled down the monastery church and rebuilt it. It was a time of scarcity, and the greedy governor of Mosul, urged on by jealous men, fined the monastery fifteen thousand dirhams.[4] About the same time, one Hujair, a believer of noble family, built a monastery, which he named Hujairabad. The metropolitan refused to consecrate it.[5] In Egypt, Abu l Jarrāh Bishr b. Aus plundered the monastery of Mart Mariam, near Bilbes, but afterwards restored to it all he had taken away.[6] The caliph Marwān plundered and destroyed many monasteries in Egypt, as he fled before the Abbasid troops.[7] He destroyed all the churches in Tāna except one, and he asked three thousand dinars as the price for sparing that. As the rich men of the town could only collect two

---

[1] Agh., 19, 59 ; I.Khall., 1, 212.   [2] S., 147.
[3] A.S., 103 ; K., 77 ; M., 2, 493, 1, 303.   [4] Thomas, 1, 206.
[5] Thomas, 2, 282.   [6] S., 158.   [7] S., 181, 185.

thousand, he turned one-third of it into a mosque.[1]
Some merchants begged him to give back to the
Melkites the church of Abū Mīna, in Mareotis. The
result was a riot in the governor's palace.[2]

In 141 the altar and apse of the great church in
Nisibis were completed.[3] In 146 Mansūr ordered
Yazīd b. Hātim to install the government offices in
the churches in the castle in Fustāt.[4] In the reign
of Mahdi, or perhaps a little later, the convent of
the Greeks in Baghdad was built.[5] Hārūn Rashīd,
soon after his accession, told 'Ali b. Sulaimān, the
governor of Egypt, to destroy the newly-built
churches. He pulled down that of Mary, beside
the church of Abū Shenūda, and those of the Guard-
house of Constantine. He was offered fifty thousand
dinars to spare them, but refused. Makrīzi says that
these churches were destroyed about twenty years
before, after a revolt of Copts in Sakhā.[6] In the
reign of Hārūn, Mūsā b. 'Isā allowed the Christians
to rebuild the churches which 'Ali b. Sulaimān had
destroyed. This was done on the advice of Laith b.
Sa'd and Abdulla b. Lahī'a, who said that they were
national buildings. They argued that all the
churches in Egypt had been built under Islam in
the days of the Companions and Followers. Makrīzi
calls Abdulla *kadi* of Misr. The arguments of these
two do more credit to their hearts than their
heads.[7]

The convent of Samālu was built in Baghdad
about this time.[8] Hārūn helped the Melkites to

[1] A.S., 222.   [2] S., 167.   [3] Elias, 128.   [4] K., 115.
[5] Y., 2, 662.   [6] K., 131 ; M., 2, 493.   [7] K., 132 ; M., 2, 493.
[8] Y., 2, 670.

recover some churches which the Copts had seized.[1]
In 191 he destroyed some in al 'Awāsim, the frontier
province, and used the material of two of them to
build the town of Hadath.[2]   His action here may
have been due to the fact that the Christians of the
province were helping the Greeks.   Bishop Anania
built a monastery on the site of a ruined castle,
which he bought from the Arabs.[3]

About the year 198 Ibrāhīm of Kuraish, the prefect
of Harrān, was walking in his lofty palace and saw
some new buildings. He asked his cup-bearers what
these new white buildings were. They said, ' New
churches, which the Christians have built in your
time ; wherefor many of the Arabs are vexed that
you should have allowed them to build what had
not been built before.' He ordered every new church
to be pulled down before the sun set. At once they
destroyed the altar of the Catholic Church and that
of the Theotokos, part of that of Mar George, and
others of the Chalcedonians and Nestorians, and
synagogues of the Jews. When morning dawned
God had changed his mind, and he permitted what
had been destroyed to be restored gradually. They
were quickly rebuilt.[4]

During the fighting between Amīn and Māmūn
many monasteries in the Wādi Habīb (Wādi Natrun)
were destroyed, but were rebuilt a few years later.[5]
Some chamberlains of Māmūn restored the church
of the Virgin at al Kantara, and two servants
(*farrāsh*) obtained permission to build one on Mount
Mukattam, because those in the castle were too far

---

[1] Eut., 2, 410 ; M., 2, 493.   [2] T., III, 712 ; Lang., 263.
[3] Lang., 266.   [4] S.A., 2, 10 ; B.H., 139.   [5] M., 2, 492 f.

away.[1] In this reign Bukām, a wealthy Christian of
Būra, built many beautiful churches in his native
town.[2]

If the *Kitāb ul Umm* represents the opinions of
Shāfe'i, and not those of his disciples, by the year
200 it was recognized that churches might not be
built in towns where Muslims lived, though in
places where there were none Christians could build
churches as they pleased and celebrate their festivals.[3]

The Muslims were not always as tactful as they
might have been. It is recorded that one of
them shut up his dog for the night in the outer
martyrium, close by the church.[4]

Arabs gathered from Harrān, Edessa and Samo-
sata, to ask 'Abdulla b. Tāhir to destroy the churches
which had been built during the last ten years or so.
He refused, saying, ' The poor Christians have not rebuilt one-tenth of the churches which have been
ruined and burnt.' In his days, adds the chronicler,
the Christians enjoyed peace and prosperity.[5]
Muhammad, the brother of 'Abdulla, gave orders to
destroy the churches in Beth Nahrain. Dionysius,
the patriarch, and his brother Theodosius, metropolitan of Edessa, went down to Egypt to 'Abdulla,
and brought back orders to stop this persecution.[6]
When 'Abdulla (the text has 'Ubaidulla) b. Tāhir
returned from Egypt, on his way to Baghdad, the
Muslims of Jerusalem complained that the Christians had transgressed and done what was not lawful
for them. They had pulled down the dome of the
Church of the Resurrection, and enlarged it so that

---

[1] A.S., 154 ; Eut., 2, 430.   [2] Eut., 2, 434.   [3] Umm, 4, 126.
[4] Thomas, 1, 229.   [5] S.A., 2, 16.   [6] S.A., 2, 21, 271.

4

it was higher than the Dome of the Rock. 'Abdulla put the patriarch Thomas and some of his companions in prison, to enquire into this matter. Had the complaint been true he would have had them flogged. A Muslim came to them in prison by night, and said to Thomas, 'If I tell you an argument that will save you, your companions, and the dome, will you pay me, and my children after me, a thousand dinars yearly from the revenues of the church?' The patriarch gave the promise in writing, and the Muslim said, 'Ask the complainants to tell the height of the old dome and of the new.' They could not do this, so Thomas and his friends were released.[1] About this time a church was built in Jerusalem for visitors from Egypt.[2]

In 239 Mutawakkil ordered all new churches to be destroyed.[3] From this survey certain facts are clear. At first churches were built freely, sometimes with the approval or even the help of authority. 'Umar II is said to have forbidden the building of churches. As only one historian records this, and the Christian records are silent, it may not be true. Apart from this solitary notice, it is not till 150 or 170 that there is the least suggestion of a ban on new churches, and this idea was slow in finding general recognition. Mutawakkil was the first to make this ban law. On the other hand, from an early date churches were always liable to be destroyed for some caprice of the ruler. In times of political upheaval the danger was of course greater. Usually much, if not everything, depended on the

[1] Eut., 2, 455.   [2] M., 2, 494.   [3] T., III, 1419.

character of the ruler, were he governor or caliph. One thing is certain, the first century of Islam knew nothing about the covenant of 'Umar.

In the second century the idea began to take shape that all places of worship had been built under Islam. Later this became the general view.

The law of Mutawakkil was not the end of the story: sometimes it was enforced and sometimes not. Sometimes the mob took the law into its own hands. It is enough to make a list of riots in which religious buildings were destroyed.

In 271 or 272 the convent of Kalilishu, in Baghdad, was destroyed, the gold and silver vessels stolen, and all wood in the building sold.[1] The last item is explained by the scarcity of wood in Mesopotamia.

In 312 the church and convent of Mary, in Damascus, were burnt and plundered, and other churches wrecked.[2] A little later two Melkite churches in Ramleh, Kosmas and Cyriac, and others in Ascalon and Cæsarea, were destroyed. Complaint was made to Muktadir, who gave orders to repair the damage. In 321 the church outside the fort at Tinnīs was destroyed. Then the Christians rebuilt the church in the town, but when it was nearly finished the Muslims burnt and destroyed it. The sultan helped in rebuilding it.[3] In 325 the eastern gates and half the cloister of the Church of the Resurrection, in Jerusalem, were burnt and the church sacked.[4] A year or two later the Muslims, helped by the Jews, sacked and burnt the Church of the Dark

---

[1] Elias, 68 ; T., III, 2107.   [2] M., 2, 494.   [3] Eut., 2, 513.
[4] Eut., 2, 529 ; M., 2, 495.

Madonna, in Ascalon. The bishop fled to Ramleh and died there.[1] In 355 the Church of the Holy Sepulchre was burnt. Kāfūr wrote to the emperor, who was invading Syria, that he might restore it.[2] In 392, during an anti-Christian riot in Baghdad, houses were plundered and churches attacked. A Jacobite church was set on fire, and it fell on a crowd of Muslims, killing men, women and children.[3] Many churches were ruined during the invasion of of Egypt by Asad ud Dīn Shirkuh ;[4] but this is not surprising, for one object of the invasion was to overthrow the Fatimid heresy, and passions had been further inflamed by the presence of the Franks in Egypt. In his book on the churches of Egypt, Abū Sālih often refers to the destruction of churches and monasteries.

The behaviour of the government varied. In 240 the inhabitants of Hims, with the help of the Christians, started a riot against the governor. So Mutawakkil ordered the Christians to be expelled from the town and their churches destroyed. One, that adjoined the mosque, was incorporated into it. In the circumstances, these drastic measures seem natural.[5] Eutychius laments that in his day the Muslims met in the church at Bethlehem for prayers, and had removed the mosaics and put up their own inscriptions. They also met for prayers on the steps of the Church of Constantine, all contrary to the treaty of 'Umar.[6] When building that quarter of Cairo known as Katāi', Ahmad b. Tūlūn ploughed up Jewish and Christian ceme-

---

[1] M., 2, 495.   [2] Ecl., 2, 221 n.   [3] Ecl., 3, 418 ; B.H., 203.
[4] E.g. A.S., 91, 250.   [5] T., III, 1423 ; B., 134.   [6] Eut., 2, 290.

teries.[1] In 328 the ruler of Egypt sent an officer
to seal the doors of the Melkite churches in Tinnīs,
and bring the sacramental vessels to Fustāt. The
patriarch redeemed them for five thousand dinars,
and to get the money sold the church estates.[2] In
350 the Church of Mar Behnām, in Tripoli, of Syria,
was built.[3] In 369 the vizier Nasr b. Hārūn was
given permission to build churches and monasteries.[4]

Sometimes the authorities made a show of
observing legal forms. Al Kindi has preserved an
account of one such episode; here it is. 'It
happened that one side of the Church of Abū
Shenūda fell, and the Christians offered much
money to be allowed to restore it. Lawyers'
opinion was asked. Ibn Haddād said that it should
be destroyed, and the school of Mālik agreed with
him, but Muhammad b. 'Ali said that it might be
restored and rebuilt. The crowd raised a tumult
against him, and wanted to burn his house, so he
hid himself. The mob surrounded the church.
When the governor heard of it he was angry, and
sent his chief retainers with many men ; the crowd,
however, stoned them. The governor was informed,
so he sent Ibn Haddād with the command, "Ride
to the church ; if it still stands, let it be ; if it is in
ruins, pull it down ". He came with 'Ali b. 'Abdulla
b. Nuwās, the engineer, and met a dense crowd. He
spoke kindly and pleasantly to them, told them that
he was on their side, till they cleared the road and
he could enter the church. He drove out all the
Christians, shut the doors, and gave the engineer a

---

[1] M., 1, 315.   [2] M., 2, 495.   [3] B.H., 184.   [4] Ecl., 2, 408.

candle. He went into the sanctuary[1] and examined it, and gave his report. "It will last fifteen years, and then part will fall; it will then last forty, and all will fall." So it was left and not rebuilt. In 366 it was rebuilt.'[2]

The caliph al 'Azīz gave orders that the Church of Mercurius should be restored to the patriarch. The common people attacked the patriarch and hindered him from rebuilding it. Al 'Azīz offered money for the work, which was refused, but a guard for the workmen was accepted.[3]

Al Hākim biamr illah gave orders that the churches in his dominions should be destroyed. Their contents were seized and the vessels of gold and silver sold in the markets. In the church of the Mu'allaka was a great store of goldsmith's work and fine cloth. Muslim prayers were said in Abū Shenūda. The church lands were confiscated, and every one who asked for some got it. A Muslim historian reports that over thirty thousand churches, which had been built by the Greeks, were destroyed in Egypt, Syria and elsewhere. Bar Hebræus is more modest, he only says thousands. Among them was the Church of the Resurrection, at Jerusalem; it was destroyed ' to the roots ', and everything in it stolen. The chief damage was done between 403 and 405, though one account puts the Jerusalem trouble in 400. When the monastery of Kusair, in Egypt, was destroyed, in 400, the common people stole the timbers from the ruins, and even the coffins of the dead. Al Hākim changed his mind before his

---

[1] *Madbah* usually means ' altar ', but here ' sanctuary '.
[2] K., 554.   [3] A.S., 117.

death, and suffered the Christians to rebuild their
places of worship. They did so, and made them finer
than before. Another account says that they were
shut for nine years.[1]

In 418 the caliph az Zāhir allowed the Church of
the Resurrection to be restored, in return for the
restoration of a mosque in Constantinople.[2] In 439
the patriarch built the Church of Bu Markura, in
Cairo, and that of Our Lady in the quarter of the
Greeks.[3] In the reign of Mustansir (427–487), during
disturbances in Upper Egypt, the monks of a monastery near Ushmunain were killed.[4] In the same
reign the Church of George, in Hamrā, was restored.
It was destroyed when the Kurds entered Egypt,
and restored in the following year along with others.
The mob was annoyed, sacked and wrecked it. The
property was given back and it was consecrated
afresh.[5] The caliphs Hāfiz, Zāfir, and 'Adid contri-
buted to the support of the Church of al Martūti.[6]

Al Bustān was allotted as a fief to the canon
lawyer Bahā ud Dīn 'Ali, who set apart for the
Armenians the Church of John the Baptist in the
Zuwaila quarter; here the patriarch dwelt in 564.
By a decree of the sultan, the Copts took possession
of this church. Then certain Christians allowed
their servants to beat the Muslim guardians of it.
These complained to Bahā ud Dīn 'Ali. He told the
sultan, who took back the decree empowering the
Copts to hold the church. Not long after, in 573, he
issued a fresh decree restoring it to them.[7]

[1] B.H., 204 f. ; M., 2, 287, 494 ; Ath., y. 398 ; A.S., 142, 147 ; A.M., II,
2, 65 ; Husn, 2, 168.
[2] M., 1, 355.   [3] M., 2, 496.   [4] A.S., 252.   [5] A.S., 91.
[6] A.S., 140.   [7] A.S., 3-11.

Benjamin of Tudela found a synagogue in Kūfa;[1] so the opinion of Ibn 'Abbās was not followed in practical life.

In 573 there was trouble in Medain. The mosque was close to a synagogue, and the Jews were disturbed by the frequent calls to prayer. The *muedhdhin* paid no attention to their complaint, so there was a quarrel and the Jews got the better of it. The Muslims came to Baghdad with a petition, but Ibn ul 'Attār, the controller of stores, put them in gaol. They were let out, and came to the castle mosque before the Friday prayers, to ask for aid. The prayers were cut short and they again asked for help. Some soldiers tried to stop them, but the populace took their part, grew angry and very abusive in defence of Islam, tore bricks out of the wall, and stoned the soldiers till they ran away. The mob then rushed to the shops of the money changers,[2] most of whom were Jews, and pillaged them. The keeper of the gate tried to stop them, so they stoned him and he ran away. The city was disturbed, and the synagogue by the Basāsīri gate was destroyed and the book of the Law burnt. The caliph ordered the synagogue at Medain to be turned into a mosque.[3]

When Nūr ud Dīn Zanji conquered Mosul he ordered all new churches and buildings to be destroyed, so two churches, one Nestorian and one Jacobite, were pulled down.[4] Apparently they were quickly rebuilt. About this time some Kurds captured the monastery of Mar Mattai, in the land of Nineveh, seized all the valuables, and killed fifteen

---

[1] Benj., 64.   [2] *Mukhliṭ*, or *mukhalliṭ*, meaning unknown.
[3] Ath., y. 573.   [4] S.A., 2, 166, 168.

monks; they also took that of Mar Sergius, in
which Moses bar Kefa had been a pupil.[1] And in
Edessa the great Church of Hagia Sophia (?) was
destroyed to its foundations, and the stones taken
away to build a mosque in Harrān and the castle in
Edessa. The west wall of the Church of the Apostles
fell, so the whole was pulled down, as well as those
of the Forty Martyrs, near the mosque, and Mar
Stephen.[2] At the capture of Jerusalem all the
churches, except that of the Resurrection, were
stripped of the iron, wood, doors, and marble
on the walls and floors. Every Christian who
entered the church to worship at the Holy Grave
had to pay ten dinars to the Muslim guards.[3] But
Najm ud Dīn, the lord of Mardīn, was favourable to
the Christians, their churches, and monasteries, and
was more concerned than they themselves with
building churches in his land. Regularly he visited
the monasteries, and liked to drink and stay there.[4]
And when Kilij Arslān captured the town of
Kaisum (c. 568) he abolished the gold tax on the
monastery of Mar Barsūma.[5]

When the Mongols conquered Damascus, in 658,
Hulagu protected the Christians. They drank wine
in public in Ramadān, poured it on the clothes of
Muslims, and on the doors of mosques. When they
carried the cross in procession they made the shop-
keepers stand up, and ill-treated those who refused to
do so. They preached sermons in praise of their
faith, exclaiming, ' The faith of the Messiah triumphs
to-day.' If the Muslims complained they were beaten.

[1] S.A., 2, 168. [2] S.A., 2, 170. [3] S.A., 2, 201 ; M., 2, 234.
[4] S.A., 2, 182. [5] S.A., 2, 187.

The governor loaded the priests with honours. When the Mongols were driven out the Muslims plundered the houses of the Christians and destroyed all they could. They ruined two churches, slaughtered many Christians, and enslaved others. Thus they avenged themselves on those who had destroyed their mosques. Not content with this, they pillaged the houses of the Jews and reduced their shops to mounds of rubbish.[1] When the Mongols captured Aleppo, the synagogue was one of the houses where the inhabitants escaped massacre.[2] In 661 the church at Nazareth was destroyed.[3] In 669 the sultan of Egypt captured Antioch and burnt the churches.[4]

In 700 an attempt was made, prompted by the visitor from the west who is mentioned in the chapter on dress,[5] to destroy all the churches in Egypt, but it was foiled by the chief *kadi*, Takī ud Dīn Muhammad, who ruled that only the new ones might be pulled down. All were closed to worship for a time, and then some prominent Christians managed to have one reopened. This caused a riot. Three years later the king of Barcelona sent an extra big present to the Muslim lords and the sultan, to persuade them to let the churches be opened, but actually only two were opened.[6] In 718 the Christians asked permission of Muhammad b. Kalāwun to restore the Church of Barbara, and made a very fine building of it. Some Muslims were vexed at this, and complained to the sultan that they had put up a new building beside the church. He

---

[1] Q., 1, 98, 106.   [2] Abu l Fida., y. 658.   [3] Abu l Fida., y. 661.
[4] B.H. Mu., 500.   [5] See below, p. 122.   [6] M., 2, 499.

ordered the governor of Cairo to have this new edifice destroyed. Thereupon the mob destroyed the church and built a *mihrāb* there. The Christians appealed to the *kadi*, Karīm ud Dīn; he was angry and, being zealous for the faith of his forefathers, importuned the sultan till he had the *mihrāb* pulled down. The place remained a rubbish heap.[1] In 721 there was a general attack on the Egyptian churches. The story in Makrīzi is so long that it had better be given separately. In 755 a survey of church lands was taken; the cause of it being the proud bearing of the Christians. A general persecution broke out, and several churches in and near Cairo were wrecked and their contents stolen, all woodwork being taken away.[2] In 780 the Church of George, in Gizeh, and in 800 that of Mark, in the same place, were destroyed and then rebuilt.[3]

The information that the two churches in Khindik were built as substitutes for those in Maks shows that the rule forbidding the erection of new churches had been extended.[4] Whatever the mob might do, the government only set its face against newly-built churches. Makrīzi names several as having been built under Islam, and says, ' No one denies that all the synagogues of Cairo which we have named were built under Muslim rule.'[5] He makes no attempt to reconcile this with the covenant of 'Umar, which he mentions.

By 860, *dhimmis* had to get permission for any repairs they wished to make in places of worship. The head of a church was flogged, paraded, and put

---

[1] M., 2, 511. [2] M., 2, 499 f. [3] M., 2, 517.
[4] M., 2, 511. [5] M., 2, 472.

in prison for a few days, because he had made more extensive repairs than his permit allowed.[1]

ADDITIONAL NOTE

Muslim authors sometimes have a word of praise for Christian buildings. Thus Mas'ūdi says that the church at Hims was one of the wonders of the world, and in the next sentence he calls the cathedral at Edessa one of the four wonders of the world.[2]

Ibn Rusteh quotes a saying, attributed to the Greeks—though he does not agree with it—that there is no finer stone building than the cathedral of Edessa, no finer wooden than the church at Manbij, and no finer marble than the church of Kusyān at Antioch. It is said also that the church at Hims is the finest stone building.[3] Nāsir i Khusrau describes a church where the latticed iron door of the sanctuary was the most beautiful he had ever seen.[4]

[1] Gottheil, 400.   [2] Mas.T., 144.   [3] I.R., 83.   [4] Sefernameh, 9.

CHAPTER IV

A RIOT IN CAIRO

WHEN the king Muhammad b. Kalāwun laid out the parade ground of the Mahara (*mahra*, camels), which is near the Arches of the Wild Beasts, in 720, he proposed to build a shooting lodge on the main stream of the Nile, near the mosque of Tabarsi. So he gave orders to remove a mound of earth there, and dig out the clay underneath, to build the lodge, and brought water to the site of the digging, so that it became the Pool of Nāsir. They began to dig out this pool at the end of Rabī' I, 721. When the digging reached the side of the church of Zuhri —many Christians were in it, and near it were several churches, in the place known as the section of Akbaghā, between the Seven Conduits and the bridge of the dam outside Misr—the diggers began to dig round the church of Zuhri, till it was left in the middle of the site where the sultan had commanded them to dig, which is now the Pool of Nāsir. The digging went on till the church was isolated. Now their object was that it might fall and yet there be no apparent intent to destroy it. Most of the servants of the emirs, and the others working with them, cried out that it should be destroyed, but the emirs paid no attention to them till the 19th of Rabī' II, a Friday, when all were at prayer and the work of digging had ceased. A crowd of roughs gathered, without any orders from the sultan, and

began to cry, 'God is most great', and to use their
picks on the church of Zuhri. They reduced it to a
heap of rubbish, killed the Christians in it, and stole
all that was in it. They then destroyed the church
of Bu Mīna, in Hamrā, which had been highly
honoured by the Christians from of old. In it were
several Christians who had devoted themselves.
The Christians of Misr brought to it whatever was
needed, and paid to it rich vows and many offer-
ings. Great wealth was found in it, coin, plate,
and other things. The mob went to the upper end,
opened the doors, and took from it money, cloth,
and jars of wine. It was terrible! After destroying
it they went to two churches near the Seven Conduits. One was called the Church of the Daughters,
for the daughters of Christians, and a number of
monks lived there. They broke open the doors of
the two churches, made the nuns prisoners—there
were more than sixty of them—stole the clothes
they wore, seized all they could lay hands on, and
burnt and demolished these churches. This was
while the Friday prayers were being said. When
men came out of the mosques they found a state
of terror, due to the thick dust, the smoke of the
conflagration, and the confused and hasty move-
ments of the mob, who were laden with their plunder.
It was felt that the horror could only be compared
to the day of judgment. The news spread, and
was carried to Rumaila, below the citadel. The
sultan heard a great noise and an unwonted tumult,
which frightened him. He sent to enquire, and
when he heard what had happened he was greatly
troubled and angered at the impudence of the mob

in doing such things without an order from him. He ordered the emir Idghamash to ride, with a detachment of troops, to the centre of disturbance and lay hands on the malefactors. Idghamash was ready to start, when news came that a mob was rioting in Cairo and had destroyed a church in the quarter of the Greeks, and another in the Zuwaila quarter. News came that a great mob had risen in Misr and attacked the Church of Mu'allaka, in the castle of Shama'. The Christians had shut them-selves inside it, were besieged, and it was on the point of being taken. The sultan grew more angry, prepared to ride out himself and attack the mob, but he waited when the emir Idghamash dissuaded him. With four emirs Idghamash went from the citadel down to Misr; the emirs Baibars and Almās, the chamberlains, rode to the excavation; and the emir Tīnāl to Cairo, all with sufficient troops. The sultan had given orders to put to death any of the mob they took, without sparing any. All Cairo and Misr were on foot, and the plunderers fled, so the emirs could only seize those who were too drunk with wine stolen from the churches to walk. When Idghamash reached Misr, the governor of the town had already marched to the Church of Mu'allaka, to drive the would-be thieves from the lane of that name, but he was received with showers of stones, and ran away. They were about to set fire to the doors of the church, so Idghamash and his followers drew their swords to attack them. The crowd was too big to be counted. He feared disaster, and held back from a fight. He told his retainers to drive away the mob without shedding

blood. He made a proclamation, 'Whoever stands
his ground may be killed', so the mob scattered and
fled. Idghamash stayed there till the afternoon
prayer, as he feared the return of the mob. Then
he went away, but he made the governor of Misr
stay there with his police, and left fifty soldiers with
him. The emir Almās went to the churches of
Hamrā and Zuhri to protect them, but found them
heaps of rubbish, with not a wall standing. He and
the emirs returned and reported to the sultan, who
was more angry than before. They stopped with
him till his rage abated.

Now the destruction of the churches was very
extraordinary. The congregation was at prayers
that Friday in the mosque in the citadel, and when
they had finished a gloomy man stood up and cried
from the middle of the mosque, 'Destroy the church
in the citadel; destroy it,' and went on with his
alarming cry till he passed all bounds and fell
exhausted. The sultan and the emirs marvelled at
his words, so the sultan ordered the head of the
army and the chamberlain to look into it. They
went from the mosque to the ruins of the Tartars, in
the citadel, and found a church built there. They
destroyed it, and had hardly finished when news
came of what had happened to the churches in
Hamrā and Cairo. The sultan marvelled at the
fakir, sought for him, but could learn nothing
about him.

In the mosque of al Azhar also, on the same day
when the congregation was met for the Friday
prayers, a sort of shivering seized a fakir, and he stood
up, after the call to prayer and before the preacher

came forth, and said, ' Destroy the churches of the wicked and the infidels ; yes, God is most great, God is victorious and conquering.' He threw himself about from one side to the other, crying out. Men looked sharply at him, did not know what to think, and were divided in opinion. Some said that he was mad, others that he was a sign of something. When the preacher appeared he ceased shouting, and when they looked for him after the prayers they could not find him. Then they went to the gate of the mosque, and saw the plunderers, with wood from the churches, clothes of the Christians, and other booty. They asked what was the matter, and were told that the sultan had ordered the demolition of the churches. At first they thought this was correct, but later it was evident that it had been done without the sultan's order.

One church in the quarter of the Greeks, one in the Bundukāni district, and two in Zuwaila were destroyed that day in Cairo. On the following Sunday came a report from Badr ud Dīn Bailabak, the governor of Alexandria, that on the same Friday after prayers there had been a disturbance. When they went out of the mosque the cry was raised, 'The churches have been destroyed.' The officer rode off immediately, and found that four churches had been laid in ruins. A report had come from the governor of Buhaira, that two churches in Damanhūr had been destroyed while the people were at the Friday prayers. The wonder grew till, on Friday 16, this report came from the town of Kūs. On Friday 9, when the people had finished the prayers, a fakir stood up and said, 'O fakirs, come out to destroy the churches.' He went out with a crowd, and found that the destruction of the churches had already begun. Six were destroyed in Kūs and the neighbourhood at one time. Reports continued to come in from the north and the south of churches and monasteries destroyed during the Friday prayers throughout the whole of Egypt, between Kūs, Alexandria, and Damietta. The rage of the sultan against the mob grew hotter, for he feared for his kingdom. The emirs tried to moderate his anger, and said, 'It was not in the power of man to do this. Had the sultan wished to do this, he could not have done it. It happened by God's will and disposition, for He knew the corruption of the Christians and the increase of their wickedness, as vengeance on them and punishment for them.' Now the mob in Cairo and Misr were sore afraid of the sultan when they learnt of his threat to kill them, and many of the scoundrels and roughs fled. The *kadi* Fakhr ud Dīn, the inspector of the army, tried to dissuade the sultan from going to extremes against the mob, and succeeded. Karīm ud Dīn, the controller of the household, provoked him against them, till the sultan sent him to Alexandria to get money and to examine the churches which had been destroyed. Hardly a month passed when several fires broke out in Cairo and Misr, and the damage was many times greater than that caused by the destruction of the churches. Fire broke out in the quarter of the Cooks, in Cairo, on Saturday, 11 Jumādā I, spread at night, and burnt till the end of Sunday. Much damage was done, and when it was

put out another fire broke out in the quarter of
Dailam, in the alley of the Bride, near the house of
Karīm ud Dīn, the controller of the household, on 15
Jumādā I. A high wind was blowing that night, so
the fire spread on all sides till it reached the house
of Karīm ud Dīn. When the sultan heard this he
was troubled exceedingly, for the royal storehouses
were there, and sent a number of emirs to put it
out. They collected a great crowd of workers, but
the danger had grown from the night of Monday to
the night of Tuesday, the fire was blazing more
furiously, and the emirs and the workers were un-
able to put it out because it was so widespread, and
the wind was so strong that it blew down palms and
sank boats. Every one believed that the whole of
Cairo would be burnt. They climbed the minarets;
poor and rich alike hastened to shriek out prayers
and praises and lamentations. Men cried and wept
everywhere. The sultan ascended to the top of the
citadel, but could not stand because the wind was so
strong. The burning went on, and the sultan's ex-
hortations to the emirs to quench it, till Wednesday.
The deputy of the sultan came down with all the
emirs, and the rest of the water carriers, and also
the emir Biktamir, the cupbearer. It was a terrible
day; none had ever seen a more terrible or more
horrible. Men were stationed at the gates of
Cairo, to turn back the water carriers if they tried
to leave the city. Every one of the water carriers
of the emirs and the town was busy, bringing
water from the schools and baths. All carpen-
ters and masons began to demolish houses. Many
great houses and blocks were destroyed. Twenty-

four of the prominent emirs, besides emirs of the drum room, emirs of ten, and mamelukes, laboured at the fire, working with their own hands. The street, from the gate of Zuwaila to the quarter of Dailam, was like a river, from the number of men and camels carrying water. The emir Biktamir and Arghūn the deputy superintended the removal of the stores from the house of Karīm ud Dīn to that of his son, in the street Rusāsi. They pulled down sixteen houses near and opposite to it, till they could move the stores. As soon as they had removed them and put out the fire another broke out in the block of Zāhir, outside the gate of Zuwaila, which consisted of one hundred and twenty houses, with a portico underneath called the Portico of the Poor. A strong wind blew. The chamberlain and the governor rode to put it out, and pulled down several houses round it till it died out. The next day there was a fire in the house of the emir Salār, in 'between the two palaces'. It began in the ventilator, which was one hundred cubits above the ground, and was only put out after great exertions.

The sultan ordered the emir 'Alam ud Dīn Sinjar, the treasurer and governor of Cairo, and Rukn ud Dīn Baibars to be watchful and vigilant. Orders were issued to put a jar of water, or a great pot filled with water, beside every shop, and this was to be done in every quarter, lane, and street. The price of the jars rose from one dirham to five, and that of the pots to eight. Fires broke out in the quarter of the Greeks and in many places, so that there was no day without a fire in some place. Men pondered on what was happening and thought that it

was the work of the Christians, for fire had been
seen in the pulpits and woodwork of the mosques
and schools which had been prepared for burning.
They investigated, and found that the fire came from
naphtha, rolled in rags soaked in oil and pitch.

On the night of 16 Jumādā two monks were taken,
as they came out of the Kahāria school after the
second evening prayer; a fire had been started in
the school and the smell of sulphur was on their
hands. They were taken to 'Alam ud Dīn, the
treasurer and governor of Cairo, who informed the
sultan. He ordered them to be tortured. Scarcely
had he come down from the citadel than the crowd
seized a Christian, who was found in the mosque of
Zāhir, carrying a bundle like a loaf with pitch and
naphtha inside it. He had thrown one like it beside
the pulpit, waited till smoke began to rise, and then
went away to leave the mosque. Someone suspected
him, watched him unobserved, and seized him. A
crowd gathered, and dragged him to the governor's
house. He was disguised as a Muslim. He was
tortured in the presence of Rukn ud Dīn Baibars,
and confessed that a band of Christians had united
to prepare naphtha and to distribute it among their
servants. Some had been given to him, with the
order to put it beside the pulpit in the mosque of
Zāhir. Then the two monks were brought, tortured,
and confessed that they were inmates of the monastery of the Mule, and had set on fire the places we
have named in Cairo because they were bitter
against the Muslims for destroying their churches,
and that a party of Christians had united and
gathered much money to prepare naphtha.

Then Karīm ud Dīn, the controller of the household, arrived from Alexandria, and the sultan told him of the capture of the Christians. He said, ' The Christians have a patriarch, they depend on him, and he knows all about them.' The sultan ordered the patriarch to be fetched to the house of Karīm ud Dīn, to discuss the conflagrations and what the Christians said about their share in them. He came, escorted by the governor of Cairo, at night, for fear of the mob. When he came into the house of Karīm ud Dīn they brought before him from the governor's house the three Christians, who repeated to Karīm ud Dīn, in the presence of the patriarch and the governor, what they had confessed previously. The patriarch wept as he listened to them, and said, ' These are wilful Christians who aimed at recompensing wilful Muslims for their destruction of the churches.' He then left with all marks of honour and respect, and found that Karīm ud Dīn had put a mule at the gate for him to ride, so he mounted and rode away. The crowd was annoyed at this and rose against him with one accord, and, but for the escort of the governor, he would have been killed. Next morning early Karīm ud Dīn started as usual for the citadel, but when he reached the street the mob yelled at him, ' Is it lawful, O *kadi*, to protect Christians, when they have burnt the houses of Muslims, and to let them ride on mules? ' It hurt and wounded him to hear this. When he saw the sultan he affected to despise the Christians who had been taken, said they were foolish and ignorant. The sultan ordered the governor to torture them again, so he rode down and tortured them severely,

till they confessed that fourteen monks from the
monastery of the Mule had sworn to burn all the
houses of the Muslims, that one of them prepared
the naphtha, that they had divided Cairo and Misr,
and allotted eight to Cairo and six to Misr.

The monastery of the Mule was attacked, all
in it captured, and four of them burnt in the street
in front of the mosque of Ahmad b. Tūlūn, on a
Friday, before a great crowd of spectators. From
then on the crowd vexed the Christians, assaulted
them, and tore the clothes off them, till it became
a scandal and they exceeded all bounds. The
sultan was enraged at this and proposed to punish
the mob. It chanced that one Saturday he rode
down from the citadel to go to the great parade
ground, and found the streets filled with a great
multitude, crying out, 'God help Islam; help
the religion of Muhammad, the son of 'Abdulla.'
This vexed him. When he reached the parade
ground the treasurer brought two Christians, whom
he had caught in the act of setting fire to houses, so
he ordered them to be burnt. They were taken
away, a pit was dug, and they were burnt in it in
the sight of the people. While they were burning
the two Christians, the steward of Biktamir, the
cupbearer, passed on his way to his master's house.
Now he was a Christian. As soon as the mob saw
him they threw him to the ground off his animal,
tore all his clothes off him, and bore him away to
throw him in the fire. He shouted the two testi-
monies, showed himself a Muslim, and was let go.
It happened that Karīm ud Dīn, in court dress,
passed on his way from the parade ground. They

stoned him continuously, cried out, ' How long will you protect the Christians and make common cause with them ? ' cursed him and abused him, till he was forced to return to the sultan on the parade ground. The shouts and cries of the mob were so loud that the sultan heard them, and when Karīm ud Dīn came and told him what had happened he was filled with wrath. Now there were present the emirs Jamāl ud Dīn, the lieutenant of Kerak, Saif ud Dīn, the Bubakri, the Khatīri, and Biktamir the chamberlain, and others, so the sultan asked their advice. The Bubakri said, ' The mob is blind; the best policy is for the chamberlain to go and ask them what they want, so that he may know.' The sultan did not approve of this, and turned from him. The lieutenant of Kerak said, ' The Christian secretaries are the cause of all this, for the people hate them. My opinion is that the sultan should not do anything to the mob, but should dismiss the Christians from the public service.' This also did not please him. The emir Almās, the chamberlain, said, ' Take with you four emirs, and put sword to the mob from the time it leaves the gate of the parade ground till it reaches the gate of Zuwaila, and smite them with the sword from the gate of Zuwaila to the gate of Nasr, so that none escape the sword.' He said to the governor of Cairo, ' Go to the gate of Luk and the River gate, lay hands on every one without exception, and bring them up to the citadel. If you do not bring those who stoned my agent Karīm ud Dīn, by the life of my head I will punish you in their stead.' He sent with him several royal mamelukes. The emirs went off slowly, the order was bruited abroad,

and neither they nor their servants and retainers
found anybody. The news spread in Cairo, all the
markets were shut, and an indescribable terror
reigned. The emirs went out, and did not find anyone on the whole of the road till they came to the
gate of Nasr. At the gate of Luk, near Bulak, and
the River gate, the governor took some sailors,
riff-raff and others. There was a panic, and many
departed to the west side to Gizeh. The sultan left
the parade ground, went up to the citadel, and did
not meet any of the mob. Arrived in the citadel,
he summoned the governor in haste, and the sun
had not set when he brought some two hundred of
the mob whom he had taken. Some he set apart
to be strangled, some he ordered to be cut asunder,
and some to have their hands cut off. They
all cried, ' O lord; this is not lawful; we are
not those who stoned.' The emir Biktamir, the
cupbearer, and the other emirs, wept in pity for them,
and pleaded with the sultan till he said to the
governor, ' Take some of them, put up poles from
the gate of Zuwaila to the Horse Market, below the
citadel, and hang them by their hands.' On the
Sunday morning he hanged them, from the gate of
Zuwaila to the Horse Market; many of them were
well dressed and respectable. The emirs went by
grieving and weeping for them, and that day no
shopkeeper in Cairo or Misr opened his shop.
Karīm ud Dīn left his house, to go to the citadel as
usual, and could not pass by those who were impaled, so he turned from the road of the gate of Zuwaila.
The sultan sat in a window, and those whom the
governor had captured were brought before him.

He cut off the hands and feet of three, and the emirs dared not intercede with him for them because he was so wrathful. Karīm ud Dīn advanced, uncovered his head, kissed the ground, and pleaded for them. His intercession was heard. The sultan gave orders that they should be put in the pit of Gizeh. They were taken away, though two of those whose hands had been cut off had died. Those who had been hung up were taken down from the poles. While the sultan sat in the window a cry of fire was raised in the neighbourhood of the mosque of Ibn Tūlūn, in the citadel, in the house of the emir Rukn ud Dīn Ahmadi, in the quarter of Bahā ud Dīn, and in the inn outside the River gate, in the Maks and beyond. On the morning of this fire three Christians were seized, with ropes soaked in naphtha. They were taken to the sultan, and confessed that they had started the fire. These places burned till Saturday. When the sultan rode to the parade ground, as was his custom, he found a mob of about twenty thousand men, who had dyed rags blue and put white crosses on them. When they saw him they gave one shout, 'There is no religion but Islam; help the religion of Muhammad, the son of 'Abdulla; O victorious king, O sultan of Islam, help us against the unbelievers; help not the Christians.' The earth shook at the noise of their voices, and God put fear in the hearts of the sultan and the emirs. He rode on in increasing thought till he reached the parade ground, and the shouting never ceased. He saw that he must temporize, so told the chamberlain to make this proclamation before him: 'Whoso finds a Christian may take his goods and his life.'

The proclamation was made and the mob shouted and yelled 'God help you', and screamed prayers for him. The Christians used to wear white turbans, so it was proclaimed in Cairo and Misr, 'Whoso finds a Christian wearing a white turban may take his life and his goods. He who finds a Christian riding may take his life and his goods.' An order was issued that Christians were to wear blue turbans, were not to ride on horses and mules, that he who rode on a donkey must ride sideways, that no one might go into a bath unless he had a bell on his neck, that no one might wear Muslim costume, and that the emirs might not employ Christian servants. They were driven out of the sultan's employ, and he wrote to the other provinces to discharge all Christian employees. The Muslims made so many attacks on the Christians that they ceased to go out into the streets, and many turned Muslim.

In all this not a word was said about the Jews, so if a Christian wanted to go out of his house he borrowed a yellow turban from a Jew and wore it, to be safe from the mob.

A Christian secretary had deposited with a Jew four thousand dirhams in bullion, and went to his house by night in disguise to demand it. The Jew took hold of him, shouted, and called on the help of God and the Muslims. A crowd collected to seize the Christian, who ran inside the Jew's house and asked the protection of his wife. He was made to take an oath that cleared the Jew so that he was free of him. A number of Christians were found in the monastery of Khindik preparing naphtha to set fire to houses; they were seized and blinded.

An amnesty was proclaimed, and the people made a holiday to see the sultan's procession to the parade ground, for they had feared for themselves because they had gone beyond the limit in perpetrating outrages on the Christians. Their minds were at ease; they went to the parade ground, called down blessings on the sultan, and said, 'May God help you, sultan of the land; we are at peace, we are at peace.' The sultan was pleased and smiled at what they said. That night there was a fire in the house of the emir Almās, the chamberlain in the citadel. The wind was strong, the fire blazed, and spread to the house of the emir Itamsh. Those in the citadel and the inhabitants of Cairo thought that the whole citadel was on fire.

LIST OF THE CHURCHES DESTROYED IN EGYPT IN A.H. 721

1 in the ruins of the Tartars in the citadel
1 Zuhri.
1 Hamrā.
1 of the Daughters near the Seven Conduits.
1 Abū Mīna (or Abu l Minya).
1 Fahadain in Cairo.
1 in the quarter of the Greeks.
1 in the Bundukāni.
2 in the quarter of Zuwaila.
1 in the Flag Store.
1 in Khindik.
4 in the province of Alexandria.
2 in Damanhūr.
4 in the west province.
3 in the east province.
6 in Behnasa.
8 in Assiut Manfalūt and Munyat ul Khasīb.

11 in Kūs and Aswān.

1 in Atfīhia.

8 in Misr (Sūk Wardān, Masāsa, and Kasr Shama').

And many monasteries. Those of the Mule and Shahrān
remained empty for a long time.[1]

[1] M., 2, 512–17.

CHAPTER V

CHURCH AND STATE

SEVERUS is the chief source of information about Egypt. When the patriarch Agatho died, Theodosius sealed the patriarchal palace, so that the household could not get bread to eat on the day Agatho died. The palace remained shut till orders came from 'Abd ul 'Azīz, obtained by the intervention of his Christian secretaries, Athanasius and Isaac.[1] This was religious jealousy rather than government tyranny, for Theodosius was a Melkite. When John of Samnūd died (c. 65), the bishops did not approve of the man he had designated as his successor, and chose another without waiting for the permission of the governor. He had all concerned in this election brought to Cairo, cancelled their choice, and appointed Isaac the nominee of John.[2]

In 76 John of Sanya died, and Hajjāj forbade the Christians to appoint another catholicus, so they remained without one till Hajjāj died.[3]

When Isaac died the man chosen by the bishops was presented to 'Abd ul 'Azīz. There was some opposition, and one Simon was suggested. He was fetched and the governor asked him, ' Do you think it fit that this John should be patriarch?' He answered, ' There is not to be found in Egypt or the east one so fit for this office; he is my spiritual father, educated me from childhood, and I know

[1] S., 116.　　[2] S., 120.　　[3] Elias, 9.

his life to be angelic.' All the bishops and secretaries present cried out, 'God give the governor long life ; give the throne to Simon, for he deserves to be patriarch.' When the governor heard what they said about a stranger whom they had known only two days, he bade them take him and anoint him.[1]

During an interregnum in the patriarchate, while Athanasius was head of the government offices in Alexandria, he and other secretaries asked the governor to appoint the bishop Gregory manager of the church and palace of the patriarch, because the income and expenditure were great. This was done.[2]

When the patriarch of Antioch died the caliph Walīd would not allow the appointment of another.[3]

In return for a bribe of one thousand dinars, Kurra allowed a Melkite patriarch to be appointed in Alexandria.[4] In 107 the emperor sent a present to Hishām, and had Kosmas made Melkite patriarch. This was the first patriarch they had had for seventy-seven years.[5] From these two stories and the comment, it is safe to conclude that the appointment was made about the turn of the century. Hishām allowed a patriarch to be installed in Antioch.[6]

While Theodore occupied the throne (109 to 120) the prosperity of the patriarchal palace and church in Alexandria grew daily, till it was restored to its former state or even greater ; it was as if it had never been sacked.[7]

---

[1] S., 123.   [2] S., 133.   [3] S., 140.   [4] S., 141.
[5] M., 2, 493   [6] S., 144.   [7] S., 150.

Al Hurr b. Yūsuf was asked to permit the election of a patriarch ; he asked for money, and, when this was not given, refused his permission. Then the bishops appealed to Hafs, his successor, who told them to choose their man and then present him at the governor's palace. They chose Michael, a monk in the wādi Habīb, and asked Hafs to have him brought from there for his installation.[1]

On the death of Athanasius, patriarch of Antioch, Hishām appointed his successor and several bishops.[2]

The government kept a sharp watch on the doings of the priests. An Indian priest came to Simon, the patriarch, and asked him to consecrate a bishop for India. He refused until the governor's permission was obtained, as the Indians were not subject to the Muslims. However, Theodore consecrated a bishop, and sent him with two priests to India. They were taken prisoners and sent to the caliph. The Indian, however, escaped and went back to Egypt. The three had their hands and feet cut off, and the caliph ordered 'Abd ul 'Azīz to give the patriarch two hundred lashes, fine him one hundred thousand dinars, and send him to Damascus for acting as a spy on behalf of India. Fortunately for him, the Indian priest was discovered, and he proved the innocence of the patriarch.[3]

One Isaac, a monk in a monastery near Edessa, was visited by a stranger monk, who turned a piece of lead into gold by means of an elixir. Isaac murdured him for his secret, and then found that none of the elixir was left. He then made friends with

<hr />

[1] S., 158.   [2] S., 163.   [3] S., 127 ; M., 2, 492.

Athanasius Sandalana, metropolitan of North Mesopotamia, and became a dependent of the caliph
Mansūr. Athanasius made him bishop of Harrān
illegally, and then Mansūr forced the bishops to
elect him patriarch in 138 or 139. Knowing that he
would not be well received by the church, he got
letters of installation from the caliph, who gave him
a staff and robe from the royal treasury. He studied
alchemy, but was unmasked, put to death, and his
body was thrown into the Euphrates. Mansūr then
made the bishops choose Athanasius as patriarch,
gave him letters of installation and soldiers to
secure his position. After two years Athanasius
died, and there was a schism in the church. The
bishops of the West chose George, a deacon, and
those of North Mesopotamia chose John. John died,
and David, bishop of Dāra, slandered George to the
caliph, accusing him of having said that he would
never take the name of Muhammad on his lips.
It was clear that the charge was frivolous, but
George had not asked for letters of installation, so he
was put in prison, where he stayed for ten years, till
the death of the caliph. David was then elected
in 146 by Mansūr's wish, and it is said that when
he visited a church the sanctuary was filled with
soldiers and horsemen, not with priests. Those who
would not recognize him as patriarch were imprisoned in Harrān.[1]

It is evident that the government kept a close
watch on the church. Though the bishops kept the
right of electing the catholicus, that right was often
only nominal ; and one who neglected to secure the

[1] C.M., 236, 243-47.

caliph's favour was in danger of being treated as a rebel. The head of the Christian community had not the right to flog or put to death, though he could fine or excommunicate. He was often indulgent to the rich and those who had influence with the government. 'Aun ul 'Ibādi was threatened with excommunication because he kept concubines. He retorted by threatening to turn Muslim if discipline was applied to him.[1]

Sometimes the caliph helped in the maintenance of discipline. Hunain and Taifūri met in the house of a Christian, where a lamp was burning before a picture of Christ and the disciples. Hunain asked the master of the house why he wasted oil, as these figures were only pictures. Taifūri said, ' If these do not deserve honour, spit on them.' Hunain did so, and Taifūri complained to Mutawakkil about it, and asked that judgment should be done on him according to Christian law. The catholicus and bishops were consulted, and decreed that he should be excommunicated. This was done. He took off his *zunnār*, went to his house, and died ; it is said that he poisoned himself.[2]

The government kept a close watch on the heads of the churches, though it took a friendly interest in them on occasion. When 'Abdulla b. Tāhir, the governor, came to Kallinicus, Abiram and his partisans came to ask from him authority and a commission. The patriarch of Antioch also went there, and was given an audience before these rebels. The governor asked about their history, so the patriarch told all their doings and their opposition to

[1] Jahiz H., 4, 9.   [2] B.H. Mu., 252.

his predecessors, and that they wanted a commission
only to cause trouble in the land. Then 'Abdulla
gave orders for that mad man and his party to be
admitted, and asked who he was. He answered
that he was the patriarch. Because he was not telling the truth the rightful patriarch opposed him.
The governor then told the officer, who stood behind
him, to go to the crowd of thousands of Christians
standing outside, and ask who was their patriarch
and legal head. When he went out and shouted his
question the Christians cried out, 'We have no
patriarch and head save Dionysius.' When
'Abdulla saw this, and commissions given us by
Māmūn and his own father, Tāhir, he looked sternly
at Abiram and said, 'I see that you are a fraud;
this patriarch is the head.' Immediately the pallium
was taken from Abiram, and 'Abdulla reproved him
and said, 'Do not let me hear again that you have
worn the pallium, nor held in your hand the pastoral
staff, nor been addressed as patriarch. And if I
hear again that you travel through the land, you
are a dead man.' Dionysius returned to Antioch,
and 'Abdulla was kind to him and showed him
much honour.

Then Simeon, the brother of Abiram and an
excommunicated monk, went to Baghdad, took with
him the commission from 'Ali b. abī Tālib preserved
in the monastery of Gubba the Outer, and showed
them there. He wrote calumnies against Dionysius
purporting to come from Christians, complaining of
oppression, appealed to the commission of 'Ali, and
claimed the supremacy. Orders and a commission
were given him in the name of Abiram, that he

might go where he chose without hindrance. When
Simeon came back with this commission, crowds of
monks gathered and prepared to come into the
presence of 'Abdulla. The patriarch was sent for
from Antioch. When he arrived he was told about
Abiram, and that he had not been given an audience.
Then 'Abdulla sent for him, and when he saw the
cowl on his head he gazed sternly at him and asked,
' Why do you transgress my commandment and
wear the pallium ? ' He replied that it was a cowl for
the head, and not the pallium. 'Abdulla then asked
the patriarch, who gave the same answer. When
'Abdulla saw the commission given by Māmūn,
he said to Dionysius, ' I cannot banish Abiram
unless you send to Baghdad and get a rescript to
cancel this.'[1]

As the natural importance of the patriarchate
might be enhanced by the favour of a powerful
governor or the caliph himself, it is not surprising
that candidates for the post were ready to give
bribes to those who could help to the attainment of
this office. About the year 449 there was a quarrel
in the church ; two patriarchs were elected, one in
the castle of Mansūr and one in Amid, and one of
them gave bribes to ' the rulers of the world '.[2] The
same thing happened in Mardīn a few years later.[3]
In 688 presents were given to the ruler of Mosul.[4]
Details of the sort of intrigues that went on and
the difficulties the church had to face are revealed
by the following incident. Shahraman was vexed
with the catholicus in Kal'at ur Rūm, because he
refused to surrender a fugitive monk, so gave orders

[1] S.A., 2, 269.   [2] S.A., 2, 290.   [3] S.A., 2, 316.   [4] S.A., 2, 320.

that his name should not be mentioned in the church prayers in his land and that he should not be received. The captain of the castle of Sansun, an Armenian of the family of the catholicus, bribed Shahraman, and told him that the catholicus had a son and so was not fit to hold his office, and offered him money for his help. Shahraman agreed. The captain collected some forty bishops, who elected an old man as catholicus. Afterwards he appointed the young son of the captain. The lad took the land of Armenia, appointed bishops, and consecrated the holy oil. When Karikarius, the then catholicus in Kal'at ur Rūm, heard of this, he sent a messenger to Baghdad to ask the help of the caliph. In return for big gifts, he was given letters to Biktamir, the lord of Armenia and Khalat. When Biktamir received these letters, he gave orders to dismiss this lad and the bishops he had appointed. In this way Karikarius got back the land of Armenia.[1] These events must have happened between 581 and 589. Yākūt remarks that Kal'at ur Rūm was the seat of the Armenian patriarch; the Muslims let him keep it as they let the Christians generally keep their churches, and also it was not important.

Though the patriarch was apt to be the plaything of the temporal powers in times of peace, in time of trouble he was the protector to whom the Christians turned. During the confusion that followed a sack of Baghdad the Christians of Tekrit asked him to send them a governor to protect them.[2]

In dealing with foreign powers the government was sometimes very conciliatory. Michael Palaeo-

[1] S.A., 2, 306.   [2] B.H., 508.

logus requested the sultan Baibars to allow the appointment of a Melkite patriarch in Egypt. Rashīd ul Kahhāl was chosen, sent to Constantinople with several bishops for consecration, and brought back presents from the emperor for the sultan. Baibars told him to keep them, 660.[1] In 673 the king of Abyssinia asked for a metropolitan to be chosen by the patriarch of Alexandria. His request was granted.[2]

The patriarch was a government servant, and his appointment needed to be ratified by the caliph. This is brought out clearly in the charter granted to the Nestorian 'Abdishu III, who entered on his office in A.D. 1138. After the usual pious introduction, the caliph refers to his

'Regard for the common weal, which includes Muslims and allies, the near and the far, and the various religions of the people of the book who have a covenant and sanction of the law ; the protection of which embraces and shields them, so that the shade of kindness reaches them all, and their eyes and ears acknowledge the watch over them. I laid your case before the Commander of the Faithful, that you are the most exemplary in life of the people of your faith, the nearest of them to goodness both in doctrine and nature, the most filled with qualities which, they agree, distinguish and separate you from them, and make you worthy of receiving that which you hope and desire ; and that you fulfil all the conditions of the office of catholicus, which are known among them, with its qualities, and witness is born to you that you have the complete character

[1] Q., 1, 177.   [2] Q., 2, 122.

and nature. A deputation of Christians came, men whose opinion is respected in finding out the life of those like you, in discovering the histories of those who resemble you and are akin to you. They announced that religious men, both public and private, had examined your life, and by the experience of their need of a catholicus, to control their affairs and guide their community wisely, they confirmed and agreed, by the consent of their minds and the union of their hearts and desires, to choose you as the head of their religion, to manage their affairs, settle their policy, and do justice between the strong and the weak. They asked that their choice of you might be ratified by that approval which establishes its rules, makes valid its promises, consolidates its erection, and strengthens its pegs.

' The caliph gave orders to fulfil their request at once and to put on them the wings of desire to its attainment. The most noble order went forth—may its commands be ever bound up with success!—to make you catholicus of the Nestorian Christians in Baghdad and the other lands of Islam, and head of them and the others, Greeks, Jacobites, and Melkites in the whole land, to single you out from all people of your faith to wear the well-known insignia of the catholicus in all your houses of prayer and all places of worship, so that no other wears this dress or is permitted to adorn himself with it, neither metropolitan, bishop, nor deacon, to put them below your rank and to keep them under the place and position which is especially yours. If any of those mentioned enters the door of strife or opposition, or frightens and terrifies the hearts of your servants, or refuses to obey your commands, or from being at peace turns to enmity with you, punishment shall overtake him and retribution come upon him for his schism till his spear is made straight and his stone grows soft by beating, those like him are prevented from acting as he has done, and your law is saved from everything that disturbs its order.

'According to the example of the imāms, he ordered you to be invested with the rights of those who preceded and came before you in the office of catholicus. He ordered to confirm your position, and that of those who follow and come after you, to protect you and the people of your faith in their persons and property, to guard you well in safety, and to confirm established customs in the burying of your dead and the protection of your churches and monasteries; in all this to act on the model set by the first four caliphs towards your predecessors and followed by later imāms, your treaty and covenant; to limit themselves to asking the poll-tax from your men of sound understanding, but not from women and immature boys; to demand it once a year, without turning aside from the approved decree of the law in levying it; that the various Christians may find justice in their litigation, that he will take justice from the strong for the weak and will lead to the right him who has turned to wickedness and injustice. He will so watch over them as to establish the rights and privileges whereby men live in safety, and he will go on the plain path and straight road.'[1]

---

[1] *Bulletin of the John Rylands Library*, 1926.

CHAPTER VI

ARAB CHRISTIANS

NOT all the Arabs accepted Islam at once; the Taghlib are the best known of those who clung to their Christianity. 'Umar wished to treat them like other Christians and make them pay *jizya*, but they refused on the ground that it was beneath their dignity as Arabs. As a compromise, they were allowed to pay the same taxes as the Muslims, only doubled. Thus the tax on merchandise became five per cent. There are the usual differences of opinion as to who paid the *zakāt*. One story is that men and women paid it, but not boys. The Irak view was that boys and idiots paid it on land (crops) and not on cattle; the Hedjaz view was that they paid on cattle, but not on their slaves and other property.[1] The lawyers also differ. Ahmad b. Hanbal says that it was paid by all—men, women, and boys. Abū Hanīfa says that it was paid by women, while Mālik and Shāfe'i say that it was not paid by women and boys.[2] Another condition imposed by 'Umar was that they were not to baptize the children of those tribesmen who turned Muslim.[3]

'Umar seems to have felt it a disgrace that Arabs should not be Muslims, for he ordered Ziyād b. Jarīr, the tax gatherer, to be severe with Taghlib, 'for they were Arabs and not people of the book'.

[1] Kh., 69.   [2] Rahmat, 2, 171.   [3] T.I., 2509.

Still, justice was not always denied them. There is a tale that one of the tribe, with a horse, which he valued at twenty thousand dirhams, met the tax collector and paid one thousand dirhams as tax. Later in the year the same collector asked him to pay the tax a second time, or to surrender the horse and get back his thousand dirhams. The man appealed to the caliph, who decreed that the tax had to be paid once a year only.[1] Further, it was enough for a man of Taghlib to declare that his debts equalled the value of his goods, and he paid nothing.[2]

In the reign of 'Abd ul Malik a lampoon of al Akhtal's was the cause of an attack on Taghlib, in which many men and women were killed.[3] There is nothing to show that religion had anything to do with this, it may have been ordinary tribal warfare. At this time, however, persecution began. Muhammad, the governor of Mesopotamia, sent for Mu'ādh, the chief of Taghlib, and persecuted him to make him turn Muslim. As he refused, he cast him into a pit of mud. Then he brought him out and flogged him, and, as he would not be persuaded, he had him killed.[4] It continued in the next reign. Walīd, the caliph, said to Sham'ala, the chief of Taghlib, ' As you are a chief of the Arabs you shame them all by worshipping the cross; obey my wish and turn Muslim.' He replied, ' How so ? I am chief of Taghlib, and I fear lest I become a cause of destruction to them all, if I and they cease to believe in Christ.' When Walīd heard this he gave an order, and they dragged him away on his face. The caliph swore to him that if he did not turn Muslim he

[1] M., 2, 122.   [2] Yahya, 50.   [3] Agh., 11, 56.   [4] B.H., 112.

would make him eat his own flesh. This did not move him. Flesh was cut from his bones, roasted, and thrust into his mouth. As he endured this he was blinded. He lived, and the wounds could be seen on his body.[1]

About the same time Taghlib suffered in tribal war and lost its chief. One of their enemies announced that he would protect the pregnant women of Taghlib if they would take shelter with him. They fled to him, some even tying cooking pots under their clothes to simulate pregnancy. Then he ripped open the bellies of them all.[2]

One is glad to know that this barbarity disgusted the chiefs of his own side.

The Banu Tha'laba were also Christians, their interview with 'Umar II is described in the chapter on dress. There were bishops of the Banu Tha'laba and the Banu Jarm apparently in Muslim times.[3] Between the years A.D. 837 and 850 there was a bishop of Sanaa and Yemen, but presumably he was only titular.[4] About 183, one Simeon was bishop of the Arabs.[5] Parts of the tribes of Sulaim and Tai were also Christian.[6] Thomas of Marga, tells of a man who had been bishop of the Scattered. During a drought he had gone with his church into the desert to pray for rain. The Arabs who dwell in tents fell upon them, captured him, and kept him a prisoner for forty years in northern Mesopotamia. He was useful to them as a herd. The diocese of this man seems to have been nomadic or semi-

[1] B.H., 115 ; Agh., 10, 93   [2] Agh., 20, 128.
[3] Cheikho, 99.   [4] Thomas, 2, 448.
[5] C.M., 256.   [6] Yak.B., 309.

nomadic.[1] At times their religion made no difference to the Christian Arabs, they behaved and were
treated just like the others. A'sha, of the Banu
Taghlib, was a poet and boon companion of Hurr b.
Yūsuf, who was at one time governor of Egypt. They
were once drinking in his garden, at Mosul, when
A'sha got drunk and fell asleep, so Hurr called for
his slave girls and went into a summer house. A'sha
woke up, followed him, and, though the servants
tried to stop him, he burst in upon Hurr and his
women. A eunuch hit him in the face, so he went to
his tribe, told them of the insult, got help, rushed
on Hurr, and hit him in the face.

The caliph Walīd was friendly with A'sha, who
later recited a poem in praise of 'Umar b. 'Abd ul
'Azīz, after he had become caliph. He said, ' I do
not think that poets have any claim on the treasury,
and if they had, you, a Christian, have none.'[2]

According to the law books, Christian Arabs were
not ' people of the book'; Muslims might not marry
their women, nor eat animals they had killed.[3]

JEWS

It is surprising how little Muslim authors have
to say about the Jews ; the law books rarely mention
them, speaking only of *dhimmis* or Christians. The
natural impression would be that they were few and
unimportant ; but that is not so. Benjamin of
Tudela, found them wherever he went, sometimes in
large numbers. In Alexandria, at the conquest, were
40,000 or 70,000 of them, and it is stated that there

---

[1] Thomas, 1, 132, 2, 275 n. [2] Agh., 10, 93. [3] Umm, 4, 194 f.

was a special clause in the treaty of surrender
permitting them to live there.[1] In Persia were fewer
Jews than Christians.[2]

The Jews were traders, craftsmen, doctors, and
civil servants, and examples of their success in these
professions have been given elsewhere. Of Ya'kūb
b. Yūsuf b. Killis it was said, ' If he were a Muslim
he would be fit to be vizier.' About 380 he turned
Muslim and became vizier.[3] Amīn ud Dawla abu 1
Hasan b. Ghazal, a Jewish or Samaritan doctor,
was for a time vizier of Malik Sālih. When he was
put to death they found property worth three million
pieces of gold and a library of ten thousand volumes,
many of them valuable.[4] Yūsuf Burhān ul Falak,
the astronomer of Zain ud Dīn, the brother of Nūr ud
Dīn, was a leading Jew in Mosul.[5]

They followed various trades, and as jewellers
had dealings with kings. The widow of Kāfūr complained to the Fatimid caliph, al Mu'izz, that she had
entrusted to a Jewish goldsmith a *kubā*, woven with
gold and pearls, and that he denied having received
it. The caliph sent for him and urged him to give
back the garment, but he persisted in his denial.
His house was searched, and the *kubā* found buried
in an earthen jar.[6] The Jews of Jerusalem had a
monopoly of the dyeing industry in the town.[7]
The making of eunuchs was one of the occupations
of those in Andalus.[8] In Baghdad most of the
mukhalliṭūn were Jews.[9] In Palermo they had
their own quarter of the town.[10] Jews resident

[1] Husn, 1, 60 ; J.N., 374.   [2] I.H., 207.   [3] A.M., II, 2, 45.
[4] Q., 1, 27, 30.   [5] Benj., 46.   [6] Husn, 2, 13.   [7] Benj., 31.
[8] I.H., 75.   [9] Ath., y. 573.   [10] I.H., 85.

in Europe were well-known traders in the domains of the caliph. They spoke Arabic, Persian, Greek, French, Spanish, and Russian. They travelled from the east to the west and from west to east, bringing from the west slave boys and girls, eunuchs, silk, skins of beavers, rats, and foxes, and swords. Starting from Frankland they go to Faramā and then by land to Kulzum, and from there to Jār, Jidda, India, and China. Thence they bring musk, aloes, cinnamon, camphor, etc. They return by the same road, but sometimes go and sell their goods in Constantinople. Sometimes they go from the land of the Franks to Antioch, thence by land to the Euphrates and Baghdad, thence down the Tigris to Ubulla and Umān, India, and China.[1] Jewish scholars and doctors travelled as did the Muslims. Yūsuf b. Yahya b. Ishāk studied in Jallāda, and, when the Almohades forced the Jews to accept Islam or go into exile, he concealed his religion and went to Egypt, where he studied under Maimonides, himself an exile from Spain.[2] Yehūda b. Yūsuf was a pupil of Thābit b. Kurra, the Sabian, in philosophy and medicine, at Rakka.[3]

Jews and Christians were not always on the best of terms. In the early stages of the Muslim conquests the invaders realized that the Jews might be relied on to support them against the Christians. So Mu'āwia settled Jews in Tripoli as soon as he had captured it.[4] It was the same in Spain. The Muslims gathered the Jews into the towns they conquered, into Cordova, Granada, Toledo, and

---

[1] Khurdadbeh, 153.   [2] B.H. Mu., 423.   [3] Mas.T., 113.
[4] B., 127.

Seville,[1] because they were the enemies of the Christians. When Walīd incorporated the church of S. John into the mosque of Damascus, he sent Zaid b. Tamīm, who was over the tribute, to summon the Jews to do the work of destruction.[2] Other instances of this bad feeling, both in Syria and Egypt, have been given elsewhere; yet at times Jews came to the relief of Christians. In a time of persecution Jews lent their yellow turbans so that Christians could go into the streets with less fear of molestation. The Jews never seem to have provoked the same ill-feeling as the Christians.

Still their reputation was not altogether good. There was a saying, ' A Jew will never pay his taxes till he has had his head smacked '.[3] Another saying was, ' Do not travel with a Jew, for he will play some trick on you '. In illustration of this saying, the story is told that a Muslim who was riding with a Jew asked him what trick he was playing. He explained that he rode in such a position that the shadow of his mule always fell on the shadow of his companion's head. The same prejudice lies behind the tale that the Jewish physician, Mūsa, on his deathbed told the *kadi* to forbid all Jews to practise as doctors, for ' we think it right to kill those who profane the Sabbath '.[4] The tale, that a Jew was drowned for sitting above the notables in the presence of Māmūn, seems to be an exaggeration of the story of al Kindi.[5]

They were looked on as an inferior people, who were occasionally allowed the crumbs that fell from

---

[1] Mak., 1, 166 f., 170.   [2] I.A., 1, 201.   [3] Raudatain, 1, 203.
[4] Ghazi, 397.   [5] Ghazi, 396.

their masters' tables. This attitude still persists in Yemen, where the Jews for the most part do not carry arms. An Arab would be disgraced if it became known that he had killed a Jew. It is not the act of a sportsman.

In the time of Nāsir i Khusrau the Jews went on pilgrimage to Jerusalem.[1]

They had their own religious chief, called the Head of the Dispersion. In the reign of Muktadir, one Daud b. Zakkai filled the post.[2] Benjamin of Tudela paints a highly coloured picture of the power and importance of this dignitary, who was at that time Daniel b. Khasdai. With his ten assistants he was the judge of all the Jews. The Muslims called him 'Our Lord, the son of David'. He had authority over all Jews in the caliph's dominions. Muktafi, who restored the office, had given him this power. Every one, Jew or Muslim, had to stand up in his presence, and he who failed to do so was beaten with one hundred stripes. He had an audience with the caliph every Thursday, when horsemen, Jews and others, cried out before him, 'Make way for our Lord, the son of David.' He wore a turban and rode a horse. He kissed the hand of the caliph and then sat in the presence while Muslim kings had to stand.[3] His income was two hundred thousand gold pieces, derived from taxes on the Jews. When he is appointed he has to pay great sums to the caliph, the nobles, and the officials.[4] In later times Egypt had its own Head of the Dispersion. In 684 Muhadhdhab abu l Muwaffak, a doctor, was made head of the Jews. He was given a diploma, conferring on

---

[1] Sefernameh, 20. [2] Mas.T., 113. [3] Benj., 56. [4] Benj., 58.

him the superintendence over all sects of Jews and
the Samaritans in the whole of Egypt.[1] When the
Jews wish to excommunicate a man they blow
trumpets against him. This is not strictly part of
their law, but under Muslim rule their chief could
neither flog nor put to death.[2]

Once when a Jew tried to raise a rebellion the
Head of the Dispersion came to the rescue of his
people. He proclaimed that this pretender was not
the Messiah, and gave to the king of Persia one
hundred talents, and so persuaded him not to
punish the Jews for the folly of one of them.[3]

The rule that difference of religion constitutes a
bar to inheritance originated in the marriage of an
Arab woman to a Jew. The aunt of al Ash'ath
married a Jew, and died childless. Al Ash'ath asked
for her property, but 'Umar replied, ' There can be
no inheritance between people of two religions'.[4]

Mahmūd of Ghazna made a garden in Balkh and
forced the townsfolk to maintain it. They grumbled
at the burden, so the sultan imposed the duty on
the Jews of the town, stipulating that not more than
five hundred dirhams should be exacted from them
for it.[5]

In Egypt, in 860, the Samaritans and the Karaites
had their own chiefs, and were no longer under the
head of the orthodox Jews.[6]

MAGIANS

'Umar I was told of a people, worshipping fire,
who were neither Jews, Christians, nor people of

[1] Q., 3, 80. [2] Jahiz H., 4, 9. [3] Benj., 72, 75. [4] I.R., 205.
[5] Barthold, 288. [6] Gottheil, 409.

the book. He said that he did not know what
to do with them. Then 'Abd ur Rahmān b. 'Auf
rose and said, ' I testify that the Prophet said,
"Treat them like the people of the book." '[1]
There are many traditions like this, and it is evident
that the Muslims were puzzled how to treat the
Magians. Though the Prophet is said to have
decided the question, there is no evidence that he
ever had dealings with the adherents of this faith.
In practice they were treated much as the other
conquered religions. The treaties guarantee them
the free exercise of their religion, and that this was
no empty form is shown by the words written in the
fourth century, ' It is a rule of the Magian religion
that if a woman under certain circumstances commits
adultery, she has to come before the sacred fire and
strip before one of the priests, that he may purify her
with the urine of the cow '.[2] At first their temples
did not suffer more than the churches. It has been
shown in Chapter III that their temples were numer-
ous, rich, and much visited. They kept their own
marriage laws. In some ways they were worse off
than the other *dhimmis*. The blood money for
killing a Magian was much less than for the other
dhimmis, and no Muslim was allowed to marry one
of their women or to eat an animal killed by them.[3]

In early times relations between Muslims and
Magians were at times very friendly. Thus
Mughīra ul Ukaishir married his cousin, paying a
bride price of four or (accounts vary) ten thousand
dirhams.[4] His own family would not help him to
raise the money, so he appealed to Ibn Ras ul

[1] Kh., 74.   [2] I.H., 190.   [3] B., 80 ; Umm, 4, 104.   [4] Agh., 10, 86.

Bughl, a Magian *dihkān*, who gave him the money.

Magian customs died hard. Near Kazwīn was a village of Magians, who ate the flesh of all the draught cattle which died.[1] In Bukhāra they sacrificed a cock before sunrise on the day of Nawrūz.[2] Those who lived in Samarkand had to keep a dam in repair, and in return for this service were excused the payment of tribute.[3]

The government gave some support to this faith, which, as one of the protected religions, was officially recognized. Thus, when Bih Afrīd started preaching his reformed doctrine, the priests appealed to Abū Muslim, who sent an army against the innovator.[4] Again, when Mutawakkil contemplated his reform of the calendar, he consulted a Magian priest as if it were the most natural thing in the world to do.[5]

In certain quarters there was a prejudice against things Persian and Magian. 'Abdulla b. Tāhir refused to listen to the Persian romance of *Wāmik and 'Adhrā*, threw the book into the river, and ordered all Magian books to be burnt.[6] One account says that a Muslim divine refused Firdausi burial in the cemetery because he was a heretic. A later form of the story says that the divine refused to read the prayers for the dead over him because he had sung the praises of Persian kings.[7]

---

[1] Mas., 3, 27. [2] Barthold, 107. [3] Barthold, 85. [4] Br. Ch., 210 f.
[5] Br. Ch., 31 f. [6] Dawlatshah, 30. [7] Ch.M., 51 ; Dawlatshah, 54.

CHAPTER VII

RELIGIOUS PRACTICES

AMONG other things the covenant forbade loud beating of the *nākūs*, loud chanting during worship, the carrying of the cross or sacred books in processions, and, in one version, the setting of crosses on churches. Another opinion forbade the *nākūs* in cities founded by the Arabs.[1] The schools of law add other conditions. Thus, four things put a *dhimmi* outside the pale of the law; blasphemy of God, His book, His religion, or His Prophet. A list of eight deeds which outlaw a *dhimmi* includes fornication with a Muslim woman, an attempt to marry one, and any attempt to pervert a Muslim from his religion.[2]

The opinions of the lawyers, though perhaps not conclusive evidence of what was actually happening, are not entirely divorced from everyday life. Thus Shāfe'i says that the government must not interfere with any practice of the *dhimmis*, although contrary to Muslim law, so long as it is not obtruded on public notice. So, in a town where no Muslims live, Christians may build churches and tall houses, and no one may interfere with their pigs and festivals. A *dhimmi* may lend money at interest to another, or contract a marriage not recognized by Muslim law, and no one can interfere. It is reported that

[1] Kh., 88.   [2] Mizan, 2, 162.

'Umar dissolved certain Magian marriages, but Shāfe'i thinks that one of the parties concerned must have asked him to act. A *dhimmi* must not give a wife to a Muslim ward without the guardian's permission. Some of Shāfe'i's views are not altogether consistent with this generous attitude. He says that anyone may destroy wine, a pig, or a raw skin, for these are unclean and have no price. But there is a penalty for destroying a skin in which wine has been kept, for it is a manufactured article and has, therefore, a price. There is no penalty for destroying a golden image, as the material is not damaged, but if a man breaks a wooden image or cross, so that the wood is useless for any other purpose, there is a penalty. Similarly, with a drum or a flute. He does not think it right for a Muslim to sell a (Muslim?) slave man or women to a Christian, but is not sure that he ought to cancel the sale if once it has taken place. The correct thing to do is for the Muslim to offer the slave, and, when he fails to find a Muslim purchaser, then only to sell him to a Christian. A Koran must not be sold to a Christian. If Shāfe'i had had his way, he would have annulled a will bequeathing a Koran or a collection of Traditions to a Christian, and would have put other restrictions on a *dhimmi's* power of dividing his property. A bequest for building a church, or buying land, or servants for it, would have been disallowed; also one for copying the Bible. A bequest to build a church as a resting-place for wayfarers and the poor would have been permitted. A Christian might not will away more than one-third of his property from the natural heirs.[1] 'Umar II allowed bequests to churches, for which the technical term *wakf* is used.[2]

The treaties do not entirely support these statements. Abū 'Ubaida promised not to interfere with the festivals of Damascus, but in another version of the treaty is this clause, 'If they bring a cross outside a church it shall be broken over the head of him who carries it'.[3] At 'Ana the terms of surrender were, 'That they might beat the *nākūs* at any hour of the day or night they wished, except at the times of Muslim prayer, and they might take out the crosses on the day of their festival (Easter)'.[4] In the treaties with Jerusalem and Lydda, crosses were expressly exempted from destruction.[5] In that with Rai is the stipulation, 'Whoso curses a Muslim or insults him shall be punished severely, whoso strikes one shall be put to death'.[6]

Often the historians mention casual details which throw light on this subject. In Egypt 'Amr b. l 'As prayed in a church, following its orientation almost exactly.[7] The pulpit in his mosque is said to have been taken from a church; but there are other accounts of its origin. The governor Maslama b. Mukhallad forbade the beating of the *nākūs* during the call to prayer.[8]

When, in 40, Mu'āwia was proclaimed caliph in Jerusalem, he prayed at Golgotha and then went to Gethsemane and prayed at the tomb of Mary. Being a wise ruler, he took care to keep the peace

[1] Umm, 4, 126, 132 f. [2] Ibn Sa'd, 5, 262. [3] I.A., 1, 178. [4] Kh., 86.
[5] T.I., 2405. [6] T.I., 2655. [7] M., 2,247. [8] M., 2,248.

between his Christian subjects. The Jacobite bishops, Theodore and Sabukt, came to Damascus and disputed with the Maronites before the caliph about the faith. The Jacobites were worsted, so Mu'āwia ordered them to pay twenty thousand dinars. He bade them be at peace, and made it a custom that the Jacobite bishops should pay him this money every year, that they might not be persecuted by the orthodox church. He who is called the patriarch of the Jacobites put a tax on all monks, nuns, and all members of the church to pay this sum. He made Mu'āwia his heir, so from fear all the Jacobites were subject to him.[1] Walīd b. 'Ukba and the Christian poet Abū Zubaid were buried in one place.[2] In Egypt the governor 'Abd ul 'Azīz ordered all crosses, even those of gold and silver, in Misr to be broken, and had placards fixed on the doors of the churches in Cairo and Lower Egypt bearing the words, 'Muhammad is the great Prophet of God and Jesus is also a prophet of God'.[3] Later he stopped the service of the mass.[4] These statements seem to be at variance with what we read of the churches that were built with the permission, if not at the command of, 'Abd ul 'Azīz, but Makrīzi says that he dealt hardly with the Christians.[5] Al Asbagh, his son, went into the monastery of Hulwān, saw a picture of the Virgin and child, hawked and spat on it. He said, 'If I find an opportunity I will blot out the Christians from this province.'[6] At a later date Abu l Kāsim came to Insina, and visited the monastery of Abū Shenūda.

[1] C.M., 70 f. [2] Agh., 4, 185. [3] S., 121. [4] S., 126.
[5] M., 2, 492. [6] S., 134.

He and a concubine rode to the monastery on horseback. He proposed to ride into the church, but the abbot tried to prevent him, telling him that no woman had ever entered that church and come out alive. He paid no attention. Inside the horses reared, the governor was thrown, and the woman and her horse killed. He gave his horse and four hundred dinars to the church. In the same church was a chest used to hold the service books. One of the governor's suite tried to buy it, but the monks refused to sell it. Then the Arab wanted to take it away by force, but thirty men could not lift it. Frightened at his ill success, the man gave them three hundred dinars.[1]

The caliph Walīd b. 'Abd ul Malik was one day seated on his *minbar* when he heard a noise which he was told was the beating of the *nākūs*. So he had the church destroyed. The emperor sent a complaint about it.[2] 'Umar II stopped the *nākūs* and forbade loud chanting in worship.[3] While Hanzala was governor of Egypt, in 104, Usāma b. Zaid, at the orders of Yazīd, destroyed churches, broke crosses and images, and defaced ikons.[4] Maslama, the brother of Yazīd, who was governor of Irak and Khorāsān, gave orders to erase all pictures, whether on churches, walls, or houses, or in books, and to break all images, whether of wood, stone, or ivory.[5]

In Kūfa, when the *muedhdhin* wished to give the call to prayer, the Christians beat the *nākūs* in the church which Khālid ul Kasri had built

[1] S., 154.   [2] Mas., 5, 381.   [3] S.A., 1, 307.   [4] M., 2, 492; S., 144.
[5] S.A., 1, 308.

for his mother behind the mosque, and when the preacher began the sermon the Christians began to sing loudly.[1]

The following incident seems to be early and to have happened in Damascus. It is not possible to identify the governor, but there is nothing inherently improbable in the story. ' The governor 'Amr b. Sa'd was urged by evil men to attack the Christians in his province. He proposed to smite them and destroy their prosperity. He gave orders that crosses should be removed and torn down from walls and markets, and that the passion of the cross should not be displayed at feasts and Easter. When the governor issued this tyrannical order the Jews rejoiced exceedingly, and ran to take down the honoured crosses from the roofs of the holy temples and churches, and to demolish those in the markets and on walls. The Christians were much afflicted; so one of their notables, a pious man, who feared God and was on friendly terms with 'Amr, went to him and said, " Virtuous governor, is it just to give the accursed Jews, the adversaries of our faith, power over us, to go into our churches and make mock of our mysteries and crosses? " The governor said, and God put it into his heart, " I only ordered them to destroy the crosses in the markets, which we see as we pass by." He commanded one of those who stood before him to go and cast down headlong every Jew he found on the roof of a church. Now a Jew had climbed on to the roof of the great church of John the Baptist, and was coming down the stairs, carrying the cross

[1] Agh., 19, 59.

which he had torn from the roof. When the soldier sent by the governor saw the Jew, he took the cross from him and struck him on the head, so that his brains came out through his nostrils, and he fell dead. So this order was made less oppressive.'[1]

The church in Damascus was near the royal palace. Hishām ordered a house to be built near by for the patriarch, that he might hear the prayers and services. He often said to him, 'When you begin the prayers at night, great peace comes to me, care for my kingdom goes, and then sleep comes to me.'[2] Hishām was kindly disposed to the Christians; in his reign the patriarch Michael entered Alexandria in procession with candles, crosses, and gospels. Another marvel was that it rained.[3] In the early days of the Abbasid dynasty the Nile failed to rise. A great company of Christians went out carrying the cross and the holy gospel, stood on the bank of the river and prayed, crying till the third hour of the day, '*Kyrie Eleison*'. Their prayers were heard.[4]

In the time of Hārūn it was customary to carry the cross in procession, for the Christians had insisted on their right to do so on one day, presumably Easter. Banners were forbidden.[5] Once when the caliph passed through Edessa, the Arabs assembled and slandered the Christians, alleging that they were spies of the emperor, who came every year secretly and prayed in the churches. They asked him to demolish the great church and abolish the *nākūs*. By the mediation and advice of Yahya, the caliph's secretary, they were rebuffed and their request

¹ S.A., 1, 262.   ² S., 145.   ³ S., 163.   ⁴ S., 199.   ⁵ Kh., 82.

rejected.[1]   A few years later, 'by the contrivance of evil men', the *nākūs* was prohibited in Malatia, also the passage of funerals through the markets, and the setting up of crosses in them. A cross was allowed on the church.[2]

Mutawakkil's laws are definite. He forbade Christians to carry the cross in procession, and to read their services in the street. All graves were to be levelled with the ground, and wooden devils fixed to the houses of *dhimmis*.[3] It is also said that he forbade them to light fires in the streets.[4] When Ahmad b. Tūlūn built the part of Cairo known as Katāi' he destroyed some Jewish and Christian cemeteries.[5] When building his mosque, he refused to use pillars taken from churches because they were taboo.[6]

Under the stress of calamity distinctions were dropped. In 319 there was a bad flood in Tekrit, and Christians and Muslims were buried together, for none could distinguish between them.[7] Mukaddasi, writing in the fourth century, reveals that the ruling faith was not without interest in those whom it despised. In Shiraz the markets were decorated for the feasts of the unbelievers.[8] The yearly opening of the canal, which marked the beginning of the inundation of the Nile, took place on the feast of the Cross.[9] In Syria, Muslims recognized some of the Christian feasts and divided the year by them; Easter the time of Nawrūz, Pentecost the time of heat, Christmas the time of

---

[1] S.A., 2, 3.   [2] S.A., 2, 35.   [3] T., III, 1389.   [4] M., 2, 494.
[5] M., 1, 315 ; K., 215.   [6] M., 2, 265.   [7] Ath., y. 319.
[8] Muk., 429.   [9] Muk., 206.

cold, S. Barbara the time of rain, the Cross at the vintage, and S. George, otherwise called the feast of Lydda, at seed time. The feasts occur in popular proverbs, of which he gives examples. 'When the feast of Barbara comes, let the mason take his flute. When the kalends come, be warm and cosy.'[1] On this feast, 1 January, the Christians light fires at night in the districts of Antioch, Syria, and Egypt, and many of the common people and of the upper classes help them in this.[2]

In 330 the feast of Immersion was celebrated with great splendour. Muhammad b. Tufj, the Ikhshīdi, was in his palace on an island in the Nile, and had one thousand torches lighted round it. The populace also had lighted torches and candles, and thousands of Muslims and Christians were in boats, on the roofs, or on the banks of the river, wearing their richest clothes, with abundance of food and drink in vessels of gold and silver. That night the streets were not shut, and most of the people bathed. They believe that bathing on this night prevents illness. In 367 the observance of this feast was forbidden. In 388 it was celebrated under the presidency of Fahd b. Ibrāhīm, who sat on the river bank drinking till the time for bathing was due. In 401 it was again forbidden. In 415 it was celebrated in the presence of the caliph az Zāhir. He forbade the Muslims to mix with the Christians during the bathing. Men brought fruit, sheep, and other kinds of food. Priests and monks were there with crosses and lights. At Christmas the churches were filled with lights, and under the Fatimid

---

[1] Muk., 182.　　[2] Mas., 3, 406.

caliphs it was the custom to distribute presents among prominent government servants. In 381 the caliph al 'Azīz forbade the people to visit the Banu Wāil on the feast of the Cross, but they went out as usual to amuse themselves the next year. In 402 al Hākim forbade the celebration of this feast, and stopped the people from adorning themselves and going near the churches.[1]

On Palm Sunday the Christians of Egypt were accustomed to decorate the churches and to carry palm fronds in procession; al Hākim forbade this.[2] In 403, the funeral of the wife of Abū Nasr b. Israel, a Christian official in Baghdad, was the occasion of a riot. The bier was carried out in day-time with crosses and lights, with priests and monks praying, and with women weeping and wailing in chorus. This annoyed a Muslim, who threw a stone at the bier, though the retainers of the emir Munāsih surrounded it as guards. One of them smote the Muslim with his sword. Then there was a great riot and many were killed, both Christians and Muslims. Abū Nasr fled to the house of Munāsih, but the disturbance continued till he was given up. Then he was taken to the palace of the caliph and imprisoned for a time. He was then released, to the delight of the Christians.[3] It is clear that the relations between Munāsih and his subordinate were friendly; he was his natural protector and he did not fail him.

In or about the year 492 many Christian festivals in Egypt were stopped.[4] In 502, the Assassins

---

[1] M., 1, 265 f., 494.   [2] M., 2, 495.   [3] B.H., 205 ; A.M., II, 2, 124.
[4] M., 2, 496.

captured the castle of Shaizar, while the garrison, which consisted of the Banu Munkidh, watched the Christians celebrate Easter.[1] Yākūt, writing in the seventh century, says that non-Muslim rites were celebrated openly in Shiraz, speaks of festivals in connexion with several monasteries as if they were familiar spectacles, and of the inhabitants of the villages gathering to the show.[2] Considering the size of the churches in the hills above Mesopotamia, there can be no doubt that most of the celebrations were in the open air. He names four monasteries as the homes of four festivals during the ' first fast ' in Baghdad, and says expressly that both Christians and merry-makers were present at one.[3] In the year 664 *dhimmis* were forbidden to enter the tomb of Abraham at Hebron.[4]

Yākūt implies a religious procession at Samnūd when he says, ' On the feast the martyr is taken out in his coffin, which moves over the ground and none can stop it till it has immersed itself in the river, and then it returns to its place.' It looks as if someone had blundered, for a similar story is told of Shubra, near Cairo. The Christians think that the Nile will not rise unless a wooden casket, containing the finger of a saint, is thrown into it there. From all parts they come to this feast, riding on horses. All Cairo, in all its degrees, goes there, and they pitch tents on the river bank and elsewhere. Singers, musicians, professional entertainers, harlots, scamps, and scoundrels of all sorts go in crowds. Money is spent freely, and there are quarrels and murders. On wine alone more than 100,000 dirhams is spent, 5,000

---

[1] Ath., y. 502.   [2] Y., 2, 641, 643, 658.   [3] Y., 2, 660.   [4] Q., 2, 27.

dinars of that sum in gold. Once a Christian sold
over 12,000 dirhams' worth. From the sale of wine
the inhabitants of Shubra reckoned to pay their land
tax. In 702 the government, at the instigation
of Baibars, stopped this feast, much to the disgust of
the Copts, both Christian and Muslim. Now Baibars
had a secretary, Tāj b. Saʻīd ud Dawla, who was in
his confidence and managed his affairs, as is the
custom of the Turkish kings and emirs to have such
Copts, whether Muslim or Christian. The Copts
made this man try to persuade Baibars to change
his mind, but without success. The feast was
prohibited till 738, when it was started again by a
whim of the sultan. In 755 the Muslims took the
finger of the saint, burnt it, threw the ashes into the
Nile, and abolished the feast.[1]

On Thursday in Easter week ten thousand small
gold coins, to the value of five hundred dinars, were
struck, and many of them were distributed among the
king's courtiers. Once al Amir had double the
number struck. On this day Christians sent presents
to each other and to Muslims, of fish and lentils.
The shops sold quantities of coloured eggs, with
which slaves, boys, and the common people gambled.
The day was known in Egypt as lentil Thursday,
or egg Thursday, and in Syria as rice Thursday.[2]

In Khwarizm the feast of roses was celebrated
on 4 May, when roses were offered in the churches
in memory of those given by Mary to Elizabeth.[3]

Even as late as the time of the Samanids, fairs
were held twice a year in Bukhāra, when heathen
idols (probably Buddhist) were sold. The demand

[1] M., 1, 78 ; 2, 500 ; Q., 4, 213.   [2] M., 1, 266, 450.   [3] Br. Ch., 296.

was so great that 50,000 dirhams' worth were sold.[1]
At Akhmīm, on Palm Sunday, the priests and
deacons came out with censers and incense,
crosses, the gospel, and lighted candles, and stood
at the gate of the *kadi's* house, and then at those
of the other Muslim notables. They burnt incense,
read a portion of the gospel, and praised the master
of the house.[2]

Churches were used for other than religious pur-
poses. Official proclamations were made in them.
A papyrus reads as follows: ' On receiving the
present letter, therefore, collect the headmen and
police of the places in your district, and read them
the present letter, ordering them to write a copy of
it to each place, in order that it may be read to the
people of their own places and published in their
churches.'[3] They were also used as lodgings, for
several of the treaties stipulate that the churches
are not to be used as dwellings. We have also
seen that Shāfe'i regards the erection of a church,
as a rest house for travellers, as a legitimate form
of charity. In Spain, the emir 'Abd ul 'Azīz
married the widow of Roderick, and it is said that
he lived with her in a church in Seville.[4] About
320, Abū 'Amir b. Shahīd spent a night in a
church at Cordova. It was a bower of delight and
sweet fellowship, for branches of myrtle were
strewn on the floor, the sound of the *nākūs* pleased
the ear, the lamps shed a bright light, and the
priest, wearing the *zunnār* as a neat girdle, came
forward among the worshippers of the Messiah,

[1] Barthold, 107.   [2] M., 2, 517.   [3] B.M., 4, 1343, 1384.
[4] Mak., 1, 178.

men who had fled from pleasure and thrown off all wealth.[1] In Spain the word *nākūs* means bell.

In 755, in Egypt, during a riot the tall houses of the Christians were one object of the mob's attention.[2]

Even in the time of Kalkashandi, who died in 821, some festivals were still celebrated more or less in public. The Jews placed lighted lamps at their doors at the feast of Dedication.[3] At Christmas, the Christians decorated the churches and illuminated them. At the feast of Baptism they immerse their children in the river, in spite of the cold. After it the heat begins, so that the proverb runs, ' You baptize and begin the summer, you keep the Nawrūz and begin the winter '.[4] On the feast of the Cross they lighted fires and threw water about; low class Muslims joined with them in this game. The writer adds, ' Often the spirit of frivolity makes them bold towards men in authority. If the authorities do not prevent it, they make the roads impassable. Still, if they catch anyone they do not let him go till he has satisfied them. This state of affairs lasted till 791. Now they no more light fires, except perhaps in private houses.'[5]

It is clear that the feast of the Cross had become a public holiday. One cannot always decide what was the purpose of the public appearances of Christians. Thus in the time of Māmūn they met publicly on Palm Sunday, but there is nothing to show if it was for worship or amusement.[6]

To sum up: at quite an early date the Muslims

[1] Mak., 1, 345.   [2] M., 2, 499.   [3] Subh., 2, 428.
[4] Subh., 2, 416.   [5] Subh., 2, 419.   [6] B.H. Mu., 239.

8

disliked the public display of other forms of worship. The many prohibitions of this display prove that the covenant of 'Umar was either unknown or disregarded. 'Umar II and Mutawakkil tried to suppress the commonest manifestations of Christianity but did not succeed. In the time of Hārūn it was felt that the right of the Christians to take out some religious processions was too ancient to be assailed, however great the annoyance of the Muslims. Normally, festivals were occasions of rejoicing in which all joined eagerly. However, the *dhimmis* were never safe from arbitrary acts of the ill-disposed, whether they were their rulers or fellow-subjects.

CHAPTER VIII

DRESS

ACCORDING to the covenant, 'Umar ordered the *dhimmis* to wear the *zunnār*, and forbade them to be like the Muslims in dress and the saddles they used. Abū Yūsuf († 182) ascribes these ordinances to 'Umar, and Ibn 'Abd ul Hakam († 257) states that he ordered the Christians to wear the girdle and to cut the hair short in front. The treaties given by Tabari and Balādhuri do not mention dress. If, as is argued by Caetani[1] in the case of Jerusalem, these treaties are later fabrications, the absence of any mention of dress makes one suspect even more strongly that 'Umar did not issue the commands.

The object of the rules about dress was to distinguish the Christian from the Arab; this is definitely stated by both Abū Yūsuf and Ibn 'Abd ul Hakam,[2] two of the earliest writers whose works have come down to us. At the time of the conquest there was no need to command the Christians to dress differently from the Arabs; they did so. It was only later, as the Arabs grew civilized, that there was any temptation for their subjects to imitate their costume.

The historians do not often speak of the dress of the *dhimmis*, but a few details are given. The Christian poet al Akhtal wore silk, with a gold cross round his neck, and rode to the gate of a

---

[1] Caetani, y. 17, § 175.   [2] Kh., 72 ; Hakam, 151.

mosque on a horse,[1] and in this guise he came into the presence of the caliph. He died in 95. In 89 the Muslims came to terms with the Jarājima, who lived in the mountains of Syria. One of the conditions was that these people should wear Muslim dress.[2] In Egypt, when the Arabs wished to insult the patriarch Isaac, they threatened to put on him Jewish clothes, smear his face with ashes, and parade him through the town.[3]

'Umar II issued laws about dress. There are several accounts of his edict or edicts. According to that in the *'Ikd ul Farīd*, he forbade all *dhimmis* to wear turbans or to be like the Muslims in dress.[4] Bar Hebræus[5] says that he forbade Christians to wear the dress of soldiers, i.e. Arabs. Another Syriac author says that he forbade them to use riding saddles on horses.[6] Abū Yūsuf repeats the prohibition of riding saddles, and adds that their women must use a pack saddle when riding a camel. He gives further details about clothes. 'Umar II forbade them to wear the *kubā* (the short Persian jacket), silk garments, and a special kind of cloak, *'isb*; he complained that they omitted to wear the girdle, did wear turbans, and let their hair grow long.[7] According to Ibn 'Asākir, he forbade them to appear in public unless they had cut the hair on the forehead short and wore girdles of leather. He forbade the *kubā*, the *tailasān* (a veil thrown over the turban), trousers of some special cut (*dātu khadama*), sandals with straps, and riding saddles.[8] It is recorded that the Banu Tha'laba[9]

---

[1] Agh., 7, 169, 178.   [2] B., 161.   [3] S., 118.   [4] V., 2, 339.
[5] B.H., 117.   [6] S.A., 1, 307.   [7] Kh., 73.
[8] I.A., 1, 180; Umar, 166.   [9] Must., 1, 125.

came to him and said they were Christians, and asked what they were to do. He sent for a barber, cut the hair on their foreheads, cut strips from their mantles to make girdles, and told them to use only pack saddles and to ride sideways. In 216 the pagans of Harrān still wore the *kubā* and long hair.[1]

It is worth noting that Abū Yūsuf, in reporting the edict of 'Umar II, and Ibn 'Abd ul Hakam, do not use the word *zunnār*; they use the word *mintak*. In describing the ordinances of 'Umar I, Abū Yūsuf uses *zunnār*, but in the plural *zunnārāt*, instead of the broken plural *zanānīr*, which afterwards became common. He seems not to quote the exact words of 'Umar II, but to use his own terms. Later on, a garment called *mintak* was forbidden to the *dhimmis* by Mutawakkil. It is clear that the word *zunnār* was only slowly appropriated to the girdle that was the distinctive mark of the Jew and Christian. The word is Greek, came into Arabic probably through Aramaic, and finally became so identified with the *dhimmis* that in modern Arabic it denotes the Jew's lovelocks, the corners of the head which he is forbidden to shave.

By the time of the caliph Hārūn it was expected that they would wear a thick cord as a girdle, a quilted (*mudarraba*) *kalansuwa* (a tall cap), twisted thongs on the sandals, and shoes different from those of the Muslims. Their saddles had to have two wooden balls as big as pomegranates on the back, and the women had to use pack saddles when riding on camels.[2] Some of these rules may have been fifty years old, for about 130 the bishops in

---

[1] Fih., 320.   [2] Kh., 72.

Egypt wore the *kalansuwa*.[1] During the fighting in Egypt that led to the death of Marwān and the fall of his dynasty, the Abbasid soldiery advised the Christians to display the cross on their foreheads, clothes, and houses.[2] In 191, Hārūn forbade the Christians to be like the Muslims in dress and manner of riding.[3]

During the caliphate of Māmūn a Christian named Bukām was headman of Būra, in Egypt. On Fridays he wore black, girded on the sword and belt (*mintaka*), rode on a palfrey to the mosque with his officers about him. He stopped at the gate, and his deputy, a Muslim, entered and led the prayers.[4] The historian remarks that this was nothing unusual. Here the *mintak*, or *mintaka*, appears to be part of the official uniform.

In 236 came the first edict of Mutawakkil; it runs as follows: Christians had to wear honey-coloured, i.e. yellow, cloaks, and two buttons on their caps, which differed in colour from those worn by Muslims. They might use only wooden stirrups and saddles, marked by two balls behind. Their slaves[5] had to wear two patches on the outer garment, one in front and one behind, of a different colour from the rest of the garment. The patches were yellow, and four fingers square. Hence Christians were called spotted.[6] If anyone wore a turban it had to be yellow. They had also to wear the *zunnār* round the waist. When Hunain was excommunicat-

---

[1] S., 173.   [2] S., 195.   [3] T., III, 713.   [4] Eut., 2, 434.

[5] T., III, 1389; M., 2, 494; B.H., 155. T. and B.H. read, 'slaves'; M., 'men'.

[6] Jahiz B., 1, 41.

ed he took off his *zunnār*.[1] Makrīzi adds that a
woman had to wear a yellow wrapper when she went
out of doors. The *mintak* was forbidden. Three
years later, in 239, the caliph ordered the Christians
to wear two yellow *durrā'a* over the *durrā'a* or
kubā, and forbade them to ride horses. (The *durrā'a*
is a long coat of wool, open in front.)[2]

Working backwards, we see that Mutawakkil
gave precise orders about the clothes Christians had
to wear; Hārūn commanded them to be unlike
Muslims in dress; and 'Umar II forbade them to
copy the Muslims. The edicts grew steadily more
severe. Had 'Umar I any share in this legislation?
Probably, no. There was no need to fix a distinctive
dress for the *dhimmis* in his days; there is no hint
that these laws existed before 'Umar II, and several
that they did not. In any circumstances, such
laws might easily have been attributed to the
traditional organizer of the Muslim state, and this
was made easier by the fact that another 'Umar was
the author of some of them. Abū Yūsuf is the first
to ascribe them to 'Umar I, and before he wrote
there was plenty of time for the legend to grow up.

In Spain the Jews wore yellow and were never
allowed to wear turbans.[3] About the year 400 priests
there wore the *zunnār*.[4] Otherwise, Mutawakkil's
laws shared the fate of so many oriental plans. In
271 or 272 the inhabitants of Baghdad made a riot
against the Christians, because they rode on horses.[5]
In the next century, Mukaddasi reports that the
Magians, in Shiraz, do not wear the *ghiyār* and the

---

[1] B.H. Mu., 252.   [2] T., III, 1419.   [3] Mak., 1, 137.
[4] Mak., 1, 345.   [5] Elias, 68.

Christians wear the *tailasān*.[1] Strictly, *ghiyār* means the patched garment, but it is often used for the girdle.

Christian dress is next heard of in the reign of the mad caliph of Egypt, al Hākim (386-411). He ordered non-Muslims to wear black, presumably because it was the colour of the Abbasids, his rivals. He made Christians wear crosses, and Jews bull's heads, in memory of what they had worshipped in the wilderness. Their saddles had to be plain, with stirrups of sycamore wood and reins of black leather. They might not wear rings on the right hand. If they transgressed any of these rules they were punished with banishment. Some denied their faith, many went into exile. Those who stayed in Egypt and true to their religion, wore crosses of gold or silver and made themselves saddles with richly coloured trappings. Then al Hākim ordered the crosses to be of wood, five *rotls* in weight, and made the Jews wear billets of wood of the same weight, shaped like the clapper of a bell. When they went to the baths, Christians had to wear their crosses and Jews bells.[2] Later he set apart for them special baths. He forbade Jewesses and Christian women to wear Arabian shoes, and made them wear boots with legs (*sarmūz*), one red and one black.[3] These laws remained in force for nine years.[4]

In 484, while Abū Shujā', surnamed Rabīb ud Dawla, was vizier of the caliph in Baghdad, orders were issued that *dhimmis*, especially the dignitaries,

---

[1] Muk., 429.
[2] M., 2, 495 ; B.H., 204 ; A.M., II, 2, 64 ; Iyas, 1, 52 ; Husn, 2, 168.
[3] Ghazi, 395.   [4] A.S., 142.

must put on the *ghiyār* and wear what 'Umar had ordered.[1]

In 515 the Seljuk sultan, Mahmūd, forced the *dhimmis* in Baghdad to wear the *ghiyār*. Negotiations took place, and it was agreed that they should pay the sultan 20,000 dinars and the caliph 4,000. Presumably they escaped the hated badge.[2]

After he had captured Mosul, Nūr ud Dīn Zanji ordered the Christians to wear the *zunnār*, and forbade them to use saddles when riding on horses or mules. In Egypt, Asad ud Dīn Shirkuh, as lieutenant of Nūr ud Dīn, enforced the same laws; indeed he forbade Christians to ride on horses or mules. Michael, the Syrian, ascribes the enforcement of these rules to Saladin. It is reported that when Nūr ud Dīn left Mosul no one paid any attention to his laws. In Egypt, Saladin certainly had Christian officials, and probably did not enforce the laws about dress.[3]

The general laws were never repealed, but were usually disregarded unless the zeal of some ruler, or an outburst of popular feeling, caused them to be put in force again. In 682 the wearing of the *zunnār* was again enforced in Egypt.[4] In addition, no Christian was permitted to wear red[5] clothes. A pedestrian might not speak to a mounted Muslim, and Christians had to use donkeys for riding. In the month of Sha'bān 700, the Jews, in Egypt and Syria, were compelled to wear yellow turbans, the Christians blue, and the Samaritans red. They were

---

[1] Ath., y. 484 ; Bundari, 78.   [2] Ath., y. 515.
[3] S.A., 2, 166, 168 ; Lang., 328.   [4] M., 2, 497.
[5] Either red, or made of fine cloth.   Cf. L.A., 13, 404.

bidden to observe the treaty of 'Umar. These rules were still enforced in the time of Suyūti. A poet said :

> They wondered at the Christians, Jews, and Samaritans, when they put on rags as turbans.
>
> It was as if a vulture of the sky had spent the night in dye vats ; and in the morning coloured cloths were on top of them.

On this occasion the enforcement of these laws was due to a visitor to Egypt, who was disgusted by the pomp displayed by a Christian. He rode on horseback, with footmen in front and attendants behind, while poor Muslims crowded round and kissed his feet. Indeed many, if not most, of the outbreaks of popular feeling were due to the lack of restraint shown by Christians and Jews when they gained wealth and power. Many Christians were too proud to wear the blue turban, and tried to get exemption through the protection of the emirs. So public proclamation was made that any Christian wearing a white turban was to forfeit property and life. In another place it is said that the wearing by them of Muslim dress was forbidden, under the same penalties. So strong was the feeling against them that he who wanted to walk abroad borrowed a yellow turban from a Jew. Nevertheless, in Shobek and Kerak Christians were allowed to wear white turbans, because only few Muslims lived in those towns.[1]

In 704 it was suggested to the vizier that *dhimmis* might be allowed to wear white turbans with badges, as they had offered to the treasury 700,000 above

---

[1] M., 2, 498 ; Husn, 2, 178 ; Q., 4, 180.

the poll-tax. Owing to the opposition of Ibn Taimiya, the proposal was not accepted. In 734 Baghdad copied Egypt in making *dhimmis* wear blue and yellow.[1] In 755, in Egypt, Christian women were made to wear blue wrappers, Jewesses yellow, and Samaritan women red.[2]

The *Mustaṭraf* quotes a list of dress regulations approved by the school of Shāfe'i ; it seems to be a product of historical study, not a record of what happened. Here they are. Non-Muslims must differ from Muslims in dress, wearing red caps, girdles round the waist, seals of copper or lead round the neck, or a bell when they go to the bath. They must not wear turbans or long coats. Women must wear girdles under (some say over) the skirt, a seal round the neck when they go to the bath, one shoe black and one white. On horses, mules, and donkeys they may use only pack saddles, riding sideways. Riding saddles are forbidden.[3]

The statement made by Juynboll, that blue was the colour of the *ghiyār* for Christians, yellow for Jews, and black or red for Magians, is evidently incorrect as a general rule.[4] Yellow was at first the the colour for all *dhimmis*, and differentiation came later.

These sumptuary laws were able to adapt themselves to circumstances, for in Persia, a few years back, the Zoroastrians dressed in yellow and were not allowed to wear socks.[5]

The statement made above, that *dhimmis* had to

---

[1] Husn, 2, 179.   [2] Husn, 2, 180.   [3] p. 1, 125.
[4] Juynboll, *Handbuch des islamischen Gesetzes*, 352 n.
[5] Browne, *Year among the Persians* (ed. 1), 370.

wear a seal on the neck always, is an exaggeration.
The facts are these. Tradition says that 'Umar
sent two men, 'Uthmān b. Hunaif and Hudhaifa, to
Irak to assess the tribute, and they sealed the necks
of the *dhimmis*. This was first done in Khānikīn.[1]
In another place it is said that 'Uthmān sealed the
necks of 550,000 *dhimmis*. It is not definitely
stated, but it is implied that the sealing was connected with the payment of tribute. Then 'Umar
ordered 'Amr to seal the necks of the people of
Egypt.[2] Without other evidence, one would imagine
that the seals had to be worn always. But Abū
Yūsuf says that they were only used at the collection
of tribute. His words are, 'It was right that their
necks should be sealed at the time of collecting the
tribute (*jizya*), till the presentation of them be
finished. Then the seals are broken, as did
'Uthmān b. Hunaif when they asked to have them
broken.'[3] Seals of the years 240 and 287 are
figured in Rainer.[4] Now it is curious that an
anonymous Syriac chronicle names two governors,
Maslama, the brother of the caliph Walīd, and Mūsā
b. Mus'ab, in the time of Mansūr, who put seals of
lead on men's necks; thus suggesting that this
practice was the exception and not the rule.[5]
Severus, in his *History of the Patriarchs*, mentions
this seal once, but only in connexion with another
badge.[6]

The Arabs do not bear the shame of inventing
this custom, for it was known to the Byzantines. In
the year A.D. 500, 'after the governor Demos-

[1] B., 271.   [2] Hakam, 151.   [3] Kh., 72 ; cf. 21.   [4] Rainer, 672.
[5] S.A., 1, 299, 340.   [6] S., 145

thenes had gone up to the emperor, he informed
him of this calamity ; and the emperor gave him no
small sum of money to distribute among the poor.
And when he came back from his presence to
Edessa, he sealed many of them on their necks
with leaden seals, and gave each of them a pound of
bread a day.'[1]

Other badges were sometimes enforced. In the
reign of Sulaimān (96–99), Usāma b. Zaid counted
the monks in Egypt, and put on the left wrist of
each an iron ring, marked with the name of his
church and monastery and the Muslim date, but
not the cross. If he found one running away he
had him hamstrung, so that he was permanently
lame. Many had their beards shaved, their eyes
put out, or were put to death. Later he inspected
the monasteries, and found many monks without
badges. Some he beheaded and some died under
the lash.[2] In the reign of Hishām, Hanzala b.
Safwān put a lead seal on the necks of all persons
between the ages of twelve and a hundred, and
recorded them in registers. He put a badge, in the
shape of a lion, on the hands of all Christians ; without it no one could buy or sell. If any was found
without it his hand was cut off and he was heavily
fined?[3] This last statement about the seal and the
registers invites criticism. It is notorious that the
government kept full lists of all taxpayers, so there
is no point in saying that a governor kept such
lists unless something very drastic is meant, which
would have been worth describing in full.

[1] Joshua Stylites, 37.   [2] S., 142 f. ; M., 2, 492.   [3] S., 145 ; M., 2, 493.

ADDITIONAL NOTE

Another word for the special dress of the *dhimmi* is *kastaja*. This is Persian in origin, wandered to Syriac, and probably from it to Arabic. In Persian it means a girdle. In Syriac it seems to mean something other than the *zunnār*, for Bar Hebræus says, 'none shall be seen abroad without the *kastaja* and *zunnār*'.[1] In Arabic it is sometimes the same as *zunnār*, for 'they shall tie the *kastaja* round their waists'.[2] Bustāni gives two forms, *kastaja* and *kustīj*, and says that it was a cord, as thick as a finger, worn under the *zunnār* of silk. I do not know where he got his information; it contradicts the definitions given above.

A prisoner who was paraded through the streets of Baghdad wore the *kalansuwa*.[3] This cap seems to have been peculiar to the *dhimmis*, so the wearing of it may have been an insult. But this is not certain, for such prisoners often wore the *durrā'a*, which was part of the dress of a gentleman.

---

[1] B.H., 215.   [2] Suli, 215.   [3] Ibn 1 Mu'tazz, poem on Mu'tadid, 1, 359.

CHAPTER IX

PERSECUTION, MOSTLY FINANCIAL

THE soldiers of Sa'd b. abī Wakkās killed many monks and ascetics in Mount Marda, especially in the great and famous monastery called ' The Daughters of Five Churches', on the hill of Ras ul 'Ain. The killing of Christians is also recorded at the Abbasid capture of Damascus and during the fighting against Marwān in Egypt.[1] Evidently the killing of Christians was something out of the ordinary, which deserved special mention. These three cases all happened in time of war.

The patriarch John of Samnūd was accused of being too proud to wait upon the governor. At first the Arabs wanted to fine him one hundred thousand dinars, but this sum was reduced to ten thousand. He was persuaded by the secretaries who ruled in Alexandria to pay this, for they promised to collect it from the bishops, secretaries, and government offices.[2] Al Asbagh, the son of 'Abd ul 'Azīz, made the bishops pay two thousand dinars yearly, apart from the tax on their estates.[3] When Athanasius returned to 'Abd ul Malik, in Damascus, he was robbed of all he had gained.[4] The patriarch Alexander came into the presence of 'Abdulla b. 'Abd ul Malik, the governor of Egypt, who asked, ' Who is this?' They said, ' The father and patriarch of all Christians.' He said to one of

---

[1] S.A., 1, 245, 331 ; S., 193.　　[2] S., 116.　　[3] S., 134.　　[4] S., 135.

his chamberlains, ' Humiliate him as you please till he pays three thousand dinars.' The patriarch was made to tour the country to collect the money for the governor. Most of it came from the bishops.[1] When Alexander went to pay his respects to Kurra b. Shuraik he was made to pay a like sum, for Kurra said, ' If you have to sell your flesh you must pay three thousand dinars.' While he was collecting the money, four jars of buried treasure were found and given to his household. The government heard of it, seized the treasure and also all vessels of silver and gold, books, and animals in his establishment. He was put in prison for seven days and forced to promise three thousand dinars. At the end of two years he had paid one thousand. The monks who had secreted part of the treasure began to spend it on fine clothes and slave girls, but were soon caught by the Arabs and forced to explain how they had got the money.[2]

In the time of Hajjāj several important Christians were put to death by Muhammad b. Marwān and their houses plundered. Mardanshah of Nisibis and his son, Simeon of Khaluja, and Anastasius of Edessa were among these killed.[3]

The Chalcedonian bishop of Damascus was denounced to Walīd as having blasphemed the Prophet. His tongue was cut out and he was banished to Yemen.[4] About 160, a Christian in Egypt said, ' Poor Muhammad, he says that you will be in paradise. Is he now in paradise? Poor man ! What he has will not help him if dogs eat his

---

[1] S., 136 ; M., 2, 492, says ' 6,000 '.   [2] S., 137 f.   [3] S.A., 1, 294.
[4] S.A., 1, 314.

legs. Had he been burnt in fire, men would not
have been troubled with him.' The *kadi* appealed
to Mālik b. Anas, who gave his opinion that the
man should lose his head. He was executed.[1]

Walīd also tried to force the Christians to abjure
their faith, and many were killed in the churches.[2]
In return for a bribe of one thousand dinars, Kurra
allowed a Chalcedonian patriarch to be installed in
Alexandria. Makrīzi reports the appointment of a
patriarch there in 107, at the suggestion of the
emperor accompanied by a present to Hishām.[3]
Severus mentions a fine of one thousand dinars on
a bishop,[4] and says that a governor, whom he calls
Abu l Kāsim, made Ibrāhīm, the bishop of Fayyūm,
give him three hundred dinars. He said to him, ' I
will do you this great honour, I will make my wife
your daughter, whatever you give her will honour
her.' He gave her a hundred dinars, and it was
counted part of the tribute which he had to pay.[5]

'Abd ul Malik b. Rifā'a (governor of Egypt, 96–
99 and 109) caused all arrears of tribute to be paid.
He summoned the patriarch Michael to his palace,
asked as tribute a sum that he could not pay, and
then put him in prison, with a block of wood tied to
his feet and a heavy collar round his neck. He was
in a cell hollowed out of the rock, with no window,
and stayed there from Tūt 11 till Bāba 12, thirty-one
days.[6] When a governor complained that the whole
church paid no tribute, the patriarch asked leave to
go to Upper Egypt to collect what he could.[7] Kawthar
seized the patriarch, asked from him much money

[1] K., 382.   [2] Lang., 250.   [3] S., 141 ; M., 2, 493.   [4] S., 146.
[5] S., 154.   [6] S., 173.   [7] S., 175.

which he could not pay, and put him in prison, with
iron balls tied to his sacred feet. He was also beaten,
two hundred blows with a stick. Kosmas, the Melkite
patriarch, was also imprisoned, but he escaped by
paying one thousand dinars.[1] These things happened after Marwān, the last Abbasid caliph, had fled to
Egypt. About this time 'Amrān b. Muhammad
tried to take possession of the monastery of Beth
'Abhe and its lands. The abbot frightened him
away by sheer force of personality, and accused him
of having killed many Christians and seized their
houses. Later 'Amrān sent his private assassins to
kill the abbot.[2] It is said that Mahdi found more than
twelve thousand Christians in Aleppo; annoyed, he
bade them choose between apostasy and death. Seven
thousand were put to death.[3] This may be another
version of the massacre of the Zindiks.[4] Between
206 and 238 the Christians were persecuted in
Toledo. The story is told at length by Dozy, in
Spanish Islam. The cause of this persecution was
the obstinacy of the Christians and their desire for
martyrdom; the Muslims can hardly be blamed.[5]

Ahmad b. Tūlūn levied a forced loan of twenty
thousand dinars on the Christians. To pay it the
patriarch sold church lands. He also sold to the
Jews a church in the castle of Shama', the property
of the churches in Alexandria, and the herds of
camels of the monastery of Macarius.[6]

Further east, al Barīdi in 321 attacked the Jews,
who were the chief merchants in Tustar, shamefully
ill-treated them, and took from them one hundred

[1] S., 184. [2] Thomas, 1, 239. [3] Lang., 262. [4] T., III, 499.
[5] P. 268. [6] M., 2, 494 ; A.S., 136.

thousand dinars.[1] In 361 the vizier squeezed money
out of the *dhimmis* and then from the Muslims.
Prayers were said against him in the churches,
synagogues, and big mosques.[2] In 369 there was a
serious riot in Shiraz, between Muslims and Magians,
in which many of the latter were killed and their
houses burnt. 'Adud ud Dawla punished all the
guilty severely.[3] In 386 Bahā ud Dawla asked a loan
from a Jew. It was refused, so he seized a number
of Jews, extorted money from them and punished
them.[4] In 392 the catholicus was arrested and ill-
treated, presumably to extract money.[5] The catholicus of Jerusalem and the patriarch of Antioch
were forced to use their influence with the emperor
to secure good treatment for Muslim captives.[6] In
421 there was a riot between *Sunna* and *Shi'a* in
Baghdad. The houses of some Jews were burnt
because they were suspected of helping the inhabitants of the suburb of Karkh.[7] In 398 al Hākim
confiscated the property of the churches and monasteries throughout his dominions, both in Syria
and Egypt.[8] Isolated cases of the sequestration of
church property are mentioned. During the reign
of al Amir (523–543), in Egypt, the government
took a garden belonging to a church. The shaikh
Sanī'at ul Mulk bought this estate and devoted it to
the use of the church. It is not clear whether this
happened before or after the sequestration.[9] Another
garden was taken from the church of al Martūti.[10]
When the Kurds invaded Egypt they took the

---

[1] Ecl., 1, 257.   [2] Ecl., 2, 308.   [3] Ath., y. 369.   [4] Ecl., 3, 282.
[5] Ecl., 3, 456.   [6] Nish., 31.   [7] Ath., y. 421.   [8] M., 2, 286, 495.
[9] A.S., 114.   [10] A.S., 138.

gardens and other endowments of the monastery near Assiut.[1]

Benjamin of Tudela tells of a Jew who tried to start a rebellion. The Head of the Diaspora gave the king of Persia one hundred talents, and thus persuaded him not to punish the Jews for the deeds of their countryman.[2] Christians were killed and their houses plundered in Damascus, and in 658 they were compelled to pay one hundred and fifty thousand dirhams to Muzaffar Kutuz, after the defeat of the Mongols at 'Ain Jālūt.[3]

In 663 the quarter named Bātiliyat was burnt, at a time when there were many fires in Cairo and Misr. The Christians were suspected, and Baibars made preparations to burn them. Fāris ud Dīn interceded for them, and proposed that they should pay fifty thousand dinars damages. Crowds gathered to see the show, and the Christians and Jews were brought forward. A banker, named Ibn ul Kāzirūni, asked that he and the other Jews might not be burnt with ' these cursed dogs, your enemies and ours '. The sultan laughed, and the affair was arranged for a sum of money, the payment to be spread over a series of years. Finally, after some time the payment of the remaining balance was cancelled.[4] Makrīzi believed the tale of arson, and put it down to Christian disappointment at Muslim victories.

During the confusion following the sack of Baghdad, Malik Sālih, of Mosul, received a letter advising him to throw over the Mongols and come to Egypt. The letter was stolen, and the thief, to safeguard

---

[1] A.S., 250.   [2] Benj., 75.   [3] M., 2, 497.
[4] M., 2, 8 ; Q., 2, 16, has ' 500,000 '.

himself, spread the rumour that Malik Sālih was
about to massacre the Christians and flee to Egypt.
Those who could took refuge in Arbela. Sālih
feared that his secret was betrayed to the Mongols,
and went to Syria. But some of his followers turned
back half-way, captured Mosul, and killed those
Christians who would not turn Muslim. Many
priests and deacons abjured their faith. In the
district the Kurds killed many, among them those
who had taken refuge in the monastery of Beth
Kudida. They also attacked the monastery of Mar
Mattai, but after some fighting, in which the abbot
lost an eye, they were bought off.[1] It is obvious
that the tale, told by the man who stole the letter,
would not have been so readily believed if massacres
of Christians had been quite unknown. Saif ud
Dīn, the brother of Malik Sālih and lord of Jazīrat
ibn 'Umar, also extorted money from his Christian
subjects.[2]

'Abd ul Mumin, the Almohade sovereign, gave to
his Jewish and Christian subjects the choice between
Islam and exile. This was the reason why Maimonides came to Egypt.[3]

This record shows the Muslim rulers in an
unfavourable light. It must be remembered that
they were arbitrary and often cruel in their behaviour to their co-religionists. Their Christian subjects
were not much worse off than their Muslim. Still,
it is not surprising that disaffected Christians joined
the ranks of the Karmathians.[4]

[1] B.H., 516.   [2] B.H., 518.   [3] Kifti., 317.   [4] 'Arib., 10.

PASSPORTS

Towards the end of the first century the Egyptian peasants began to desert their holdings in large numbers, probably because of the heavy taxation. The government tried to stop this movement by following up the fugitives, as they were called, and keeping lists of them. Anyone sheltering a fugitive was fined five dinars, and the headman, officials, and police of the place seem to have been fined the same sum. The man himself was fined five dinars, given forty lashes, put in a wooden yoke, and sent to the governor. Informers received two dinars a head.[1] The papyrus 1460, in its imperfect state, contains a list of more than a hundred and eighty fugitives, apparently from one district alone.

Between 81 and 86 the governor ordered to collect from all the land those of twenty years and under (apparently this phrase refers to length of residence and not to age), so they went and gathered them. Those in charge of this business were 'Asim, Yazīd, and their colleagues. They marked on the hands and foreheads the strangers whom they found, and sent them to places that were strange to them.[2] Kurra adopted a different policy. 'Men with their wives and children fled from place to place; but no place sheltered them from the weight of calamities and the demands for tribute. 'Abd ul 'Azīz, from Sakhā, was put in charge of this business. He gathered the fugitives from every place, bound them, and brought them back to their homes.'[3] Usāma

---

[1] B.M., 4, 1384.   [2] S., 136.   [3] S., 140.

b. Zaid started a system of passports, and ordered that every Christian found without one was to be fined five dinars.[1] He was very strict. He gave orders that wherever a traveller, or a man moving from place to place, or a boat ascending or descending the river, was found without a passport, the man should be arrested, the boat and its cargo confiscated, and the boat burnt. If they caught Greeks on the sea (river?) they took them to the governor, and some were killed, some impaled, and some mutilated. So the roads were deserted, there were no travellers, and none to buy or sell. Grapes diminished in quantity and none were found to buy them, even for a dirham, as the owners had to wait a month or two at the governor's gate to get a permit. If a passport was eaten by a mouse, fell into the water, or was damaged in any way, the holder was fined five dinars and was given another.

A widow got a passport for her son and herself and went from Alexandria to a riverside village, as she hoped he would find work to keep them alive. The son went to the river to drink, and a crocodile took him and the passport, while the mother looked on and wept. When she got back to Alexandria she told the governor what had happened. He showed her no mercy, but put her in prison until she paid ten dinars for losing her passport and entering the city without one. She sold her clothes and all that she had, and went about begging till she paid the sum.[2]

---

[1] M., 2, 493.   [2] S., 142.

CONVERSION

Change of religion was a bar to inheritance. Tradition finds the historical origin of this rule in a decision of 'Umar I. Al Ash'ath asked that the property of his childless aunt, who had married a Jew, might be given to him. The caliph refused.[1] So if the child of a *dhimmi* turned Muslim it lost its share of the father's property, and, if it was a girl, the father could not give her in marriage.[2]

When a *dhimmi* turned Muslim he surrendered his real property. This was important because of its bearing on taxation. Where tribute was levied collectively—where a fixed sum was paid by the community and they distributed the burden among themselves as they thought right—a *dhimmi* who became a Muslim had to abandon his house and land to the community, but kept his personal property. Where tribute was levied on the individual the land of the convert became the property of the state. Another opinion was that it reverted to the state only if the convert had no heir.[3]

Shāfe'i held that a *dhimmi* who was converted to another protected religion had to be banished, because the protection accorded to him ceased with his change of religion.[4]

[1] I.R., 205.   [2] Mud., 4, 259.   [3] Hakam, 154 ; M., 1, 77.   [4] Umm, 4, 105.

CHAPTER X

SOCIAL CONDITIONS

MUSLIM tradition insists strongly that the conquered peoples were to be treated kindly, or at least
justly. The Prophet said, ' If anyone wrong a man
to whom a treaty has been granted, or burdens him
above his strength, I am an advocate against him till
the day of judgment.'[1] Abū Bakr said, ' Do not kill
any of the protected people, for if you do God will
require the protection of them from you and will
cast you on your faces in hell.'[2] When the troops
started for Syria he is said to have given these commands, ' When you enter that country, kill neither
old man, nor little child, nor woman. Do not pull
down a pillar saint from his place. Do not injure
the monks, for they have set themselves apart to
worship God. Do not cut down a tree nor uproot
a plant. Do not rip up any ox, cow, or sheep. If a
province or people receive you, make an agreement
with them and keep your promise. Let them be
governed by their laws and established customs, and
take tribute from them as is agreed between you.
Leave them in their religion and their land.'[3]

Various tales are told about 'Umar to illustrate
his tenderness for the *dhimmis*. On his way back
from Syria, he passed by some men who had been
stood in the sun with oil poured over their heads
(to attract the flies). He asked questions, and was

[1] Kh., 71.   [2] Ibn Sa'd, III, 1, 137.   [3] S.A., 1, 240.

told that they were liable for tribute, had not paid it, and were punished till they should. Their excuse was that they were too poor to pay. 'Umar said, ' Let them go, do not annoy them.'[1] Again he passed a house where an old blind man was begging. He touched him on the arm from behind, and said, ' To which of the people of the book do you belong?' He said that he was a Jew, and begged to provide for his daily needs and food and to pay the tribute. 'Umar took him by the hand, led him to his own house, gave him something from it, and then sent him to the keeper of the treasury with this message, ' See to this man and his like, for we have not done right if we devour their youth and neglect their old age. The religious tax is for the poor and needy. The poor are the Muslims; this man is one of the needy of the people of the book.' He freed him from the obligation to pay tribute.[2] It is hard to reconcile this story with the fact that the blind did not pay tribute. Perhaps it is aetiological, and is meant to explain why they did not pay. He is said to have given these instructions about the adherents of the protected religions. ' Make it easy for him who cannot pay the tribute; help him who is weak. Let them keep their names, but do not give them our *kunyas*. Humiliate them, but do them no injustice. If you meet them on the road make them go to the side.'[3] In his dying charge to his successor he said, ' I charge the caliph after me to be kind to the *dhimmis*, to keep their covenant, to protect them, and not to burden them above their strength.'[4] There is some

---

[1] Kh., 71.   [2] Kh., 71.   [3] I.A., 1, 178.   [4] Yahya, 54.

Christian evidence to support this view. 'Ishoyahbh, who was patriarch from A.D. 647 to 657, writes, ' The Arabs, to whom God gave the dominion over the world, behave to us as you know. They are not hostile to Christianity, but praise our religion, honour the priests and saints, and help the churches and monasteries.'[1] The agreement made by 'Ishoyahbh with the Arabs seems to have been quite favourable to the Christians. It was stipulated that they should be protected from their foes; that they should not be compelled to fight for the Arabs; that they might keep their manners and laws; that the tax on the poor should not exceed four *zuze* (dirhams) and that on merchants and the wealthy should be twelve; and that a Christian woman in the service should not be forced to give up her religion nor to neglect prayer and fasting.[2]

On the other hand, there are signs that the Muslims were not altogether easy in their minds about the position of the subject peoples, for there is too much insistence on the moderation of 'Umar. A tradition, found in several places, tells that two men were appointed to survey the taxes in Lower Mesopotamia: 'Uthmān b. Hunaif in the Euphrates district, and Hudhaifa b. Yaman to the west of the Tigris. 'Umar asked if they had not laid on the land more than it could bear. 'Uthmān replied, ' I have laid on the land what it can bear; had I chosen, I could have doubled (the tribute on) my land.' Hudhaifa said, ' I imposed on it what it can bear, and there is a great surplus in it.' But during the rule of 'Ali, Tha'laba b. Yazīd is reported to

[1] Thomas, 2, 156.   [2] B.H. Eccl., 3, 118.

have said, 'I will never go back to Irak because of the misery one sees there.'[1]

In the early days the Arabs were long-suffering, for again and again we read of towns that capitulated on terms, rebelled, were captured, and the original treaty re-imposed.[2]

No historian thought of writing a social history, so the facts have to be gathered from scattered notices.

Agatho, the patriarch of Alexandria from 39 to 56, used to buy Byzantine prisoners of war and set them free.[3] Maslama, the governor of Egypt from 47 to 62, sent seven bishops on a judicial commission to Sakhā, to try certain prisoners whom it was proposed to burn.[4]

Certain priests and sorcerers had plotted to poison the patriarch. When 'Abd ul 'Azīz heard of it he ordered them to be burnt. The patriarch interceded for the priests, so they were let off, but the sorcerers were burnt.[5] Al Akhtal, the Christian poet, was a familiar figure at the court of 'Abd ul Malik. Without permission he came into the presence of the caliph wearing a silk *jubba*, an amulet, a gold cross hanging from his neck on a gold chain, and his beard dripping wine. When he acted as arbitrator for the tribe of Bakr b. Wāil he went into a mosque and they came before him.[6] He lampooned al Jahhāf, who said, 'Son of a Christian woman, I did not think that you would be so daring towards one like me.' Al Akhtal was hot with fear, so the caliph said, 'I am your protector.' He replied, 'Granted

---

[1] Kh., 21. [2] E.g. B., 116, 147. [3] S., 112. [4] S., 114.
[5] S., 125. [6] Agh., 7, 169 f.

that you are my guard while you are awake, who will protect me against him while you sleep?'[1] Though some Arabs felt contempt for Christians, that did not prevent al Akhtal from acting towards the caliph as impudently as any Muslim poet. Earlier 'Uthmān had made much of the other Christian poet, Abū Zubaid, and had given him a seat beside his own. One of the charges against Walīd b. 'Ukba was his friendship for this man and its consequences.[2] Once when al Asbagh visited his father, 'Abd ul 'Azīz, he found Christians sitting in the audience hall, and, though it happened to be Easter, it is probable that they were present regularly.[3] It was the duty of the patriarch, along with the government officials, to pay his respects to a new governor, and it seems that his presence was frequently required.[4] 'Umar II stopped women, presumably Christian, from going to the public baths.[5]

Some governors were extravagant in their friendship for Christians. Severus tells this story: 'Abu l Kāsim loved Anba Masīs above all the bishops, and used to show him his young concubines in my presence that he might bless them. He said, "These are your children, lay your hands on them and give them your most efficacious blessing."'[6] To Ibrāhīm, the bishop of the Fayyūm, he said, 'I will do you this great honour; I will make my wife your daughter.'[7] The historian spoils the effect, by adding that the governor had the mind of a child. Hassān, who was governor in 127, loved the

---

[1] Mubarrad, 287.   [2] Agh., 4, 180. 11, 23.   [3] S., 124.
[4] S., 121, 135, 137.   [5] K., 69.   [6] S., 153.   [7] S., 154.

churches, bishops, and monks, and used to talk with the patriarch about affairs of state and the salvation of his soul.[1]

The Melkites asked that the church of Abū Mīna, in Mareotis, might be given back to them, and, as the Copts resisted the claim, a meeting was held in the governor's palace. When some men from Upper Egypt heard that one Constantine was a Melkite they sprang on him, dragged him outside, and wished to kill him. The bishops threw their cloaks over him and saved him. Severus continues, ' One jumped up, abused me, and blasphemed the holy Trinity. I and all present saw his robe torn into three pieces, whereupon all in the palace, Muslims, Christians, and heretics, cried, " There is no God but the God of the Christians, no faith but that of the patriarch Michael." ' Many were wounded in the throng.[2] There is no hint that any of the brawlers were punished.

Sometimes the *dhimmis* were treated as if they had equal rights with the Muslims. When 'Abdulla b. Sa'd b. abī Sarh (25–35) made a treaty with the Nubians, one of the contracting parties is called ' the Muslims, non-Muslims and the protected peoples ', and the Nubians bound themselves to protect 'the Muslims and *dhimmis* travelling in Nubia'.[3] The Khawārij were more friendly to the *dhimmis* than the orthodox Muslims, and they are blamed because they argued wrongly, did not follow the agreed opinion of the companions of the Prophet, but treated Arab towns like foreign towns, and let the *dhimmis* parade their religion.[4] But the criminal found no mercy.

[1] S., 165.　　[2] S., 166–71.　　[3] M., 1, 200.　　[4] Kh., 33.

One of the tales about 'Umar is that he heard how a Nabatæan of Syria had thrown a woman off her horse and outraged her. He commanded the man to be impaled, and said, ' Not for this did we grant them terms.' [1] A good statement of the principles which guided the Arab government is contained in the rescript found among the Aphrodite papyri. Unfortunately it has been damaged :

' . . . fearing God and preserving justice and equity in the assessment of the quota apportioned by them in accordance with . . . and caused the overseer with four other notable persons in your district to [assist ?] them in the said assessment. And when they have finished this, send to us a register containing particulars as to the amount assigned to each person among them, showing us in it the name and patronymic and place of residence of those who assessed the said fine. And let it not come to our knowledge that you have in any respect at all cheated the people of your district in the matter of the fine distributed by you, or that you have shown any preference or antipathy at all to anyone in the assessment of the said fine. For we know that the persons who are to assess it will certainly not disobey in any instructions given them by you, and if you find that they have assessed anyone too lightly through partiality, or too heavily through antipathy, we shall requite them both in their persons and in their estates by God's command. Therefore, exhort and warn them about this, and also (tell them) not to assess any of the officials beyond his means, even if he is at a distance from them and does not join them in the

[1] Kh., 100.

assessment of the said fine, but to treat each with justice as aforesaid, and assess him according to his means; and cause the assessors of the said fine first of all to make a written agreement, in which they declare that if they are proved, after the assessment, to have assigned to anyone an apportionment beyond his means and to have assessed another too lightly—that they themselves in equal shares will make up the deficiency caused through the person too heavily burdened in their assignment, and will be liable besides to severe punishment for their disobedience and disregard of our command; and the said agreement send to us with the register of the quota assessed for the fine upon each person.'[1]

Nevertheless the Copts were not contented; the number of revolts shows this clearly. They took place as under:

107 in the Delta.	121 Upper Egypt.
132 Samnūd.	135 Samnūd.
150 Sakhā.	156 Balhīb.
211 Lower Egypt.	

In 216 there was more trouble, and the fighting men were killed and the women and children enslaved.[2] 'From then on God made the Copts of little account in all the land of Egypt, and destroyed their power. They could no longer rebel nor stand against the might of the governor. Muslims also got possession of the country towns. The Copts then employed trickery against Islam and those who professed it, and did harm as they made their influence felt by those who kept the records of the land tax.'[3]

Conditions were especially bad in Tinnīs. 'In

[1] B.M., 4, 1345.   [2] K., 73, 81, 94, 102, 116, 119, 190, 192.
[3] M., 1, 79; 2, 494.

the days of 'Abdulla,' says the patriarch Dionysius,
'we saw in the land of Egypt at Tinnīs, and the
inhabitants told us, a shameful thing. This place is
wholly Christian and very populous, but they are
in dire poverty. When we asked how they came to
this sore poverty they told us. Water surrounds
us on every side, we have no fields, no agriculture,
we cannot keep cattle; the water we drink is
brought from a distance, and scarcely do we drink
it but at a price, a dirham for four jars. Our trade
is linen; the women spin it on spindles and we
weave it into cloth. Each day we earn as wages,
from the merchants who own the material, half a
dirham. Our labour scarcely suffices for our food.
When they levy the taxes they impose five dinars
on each house, and we are oppressed and cast into
prison. In our misery we give our households as
pledges, even our sons and daughters, that they
may work in slavery. Should it happen that a
man's wife or daughter bears them a child, they
make us testify that we will not go to law with them
about this. What is worse, before the time for
redeeming the wife or daughter comes, there are
the taxes of the next year, and we take on these
pledges further dinars. Thus our sons and our
daughters remain slaves of the Arabs all the time.'
The patriarch told this to 'Abdulla; he had pity on
them, and by the mediation of the patriarch gave
order that there should be a poll-tax on the men
and they should pay twenty-two dirhams, as is the
law in Mesopotamia.[1] In 439 the taxes in Tinnīs
amounted to a thousand dinars a day.[2]

[1] S.A., 2, 17.   [2] Sefernameh, 37 ; cf. Muk., 213.

There were, however, rich Christians in Egypt.
Even if the following story did not actually happen,
something like it must have been possible. When
Māmūn made a progress through the towns of
Egypt, in each a platform was made and a tent
pitched for him on it with his guard round about,
and he stayed there for a day and a night. He passed
one, Tā un Namal, but did not enter it as it was
unimportant. When he had gone on, an old woman,
called Maria the Copt, the owner of the town, came
out and called to him. He thought her a suppliant
for justice and waited for her. He never travelled
without interpreters, and one of them explained that
the woman said, ' O Commander of the Faithful, you
have halted in every other town and have passed by
mine ; therefore the Copts will mock me. I beg
the Commander of the Faithful to honour me by
alighting in my town, to exalt me and my descendants, that my enemies may not exult over me.'
Then she wept bitterly. Māmūn had compassion
on her, turned his horse towards the town and
dismounted. Her son came to the chief cook, and
asked how much he usually wanted of sheep, fowls,
capons, fish, spices, sugar, honey, perfumes, wax,
fruit, fodder, etc. He provided much more than was
asked. With Māmūn were his brother, Mu'tasim,
his son, 'Abbās, the sons of his brother, Wāthik,
Mutawakkil, Yahya b. Aktam, and the *kadi*, Ahmad
b. Daud. The woman provided for each one's wants
separately, and none had to supply the other, and
the same with the officers. She gave Māmūn a great
quantity of the finest tasty food, so that he thought it
extraordinary. Next morning, when he was ready to

go, she came forward with ten girls carrying trays. As he saw her far off the caliph said to those about him, 'The Copt has brought a rustic gift, spices, herbs, and wormwood.' But as she placed the trays before him there was on each a purse of gold.[1]

An agent of Yazīd b. Muhallab sold a ruby to a Jew of Khorāsān for thirty thousand dirhams. After the sale was concluded the Jew said that he would have given fifty thousand willingly, and when he saw the seller's disappointment he gave him a further hundred dinars.[2] Sometimes the Muslims played low tricks on their fellow subjects. Bukām, the headman of Būra, in Egypt, offered to build a new mosque if he were allowed to destroy the old one. The Muslims agreed, but when the new was completed they went back on their word, saying, 'Our religion does not permit us to destroy a mosque wherein we have prayed.'[3] It may be noted that when Saladin built the walls of Cairo he pulled down mosques to make room for them.[4]

About this time opinions differed about the treatment of the *dhimmis*. The author of the Book of the Land Tax could say in his address to the caliph Hārūn, 'It is right that you should order the protected people to be treated with kindness, that no injury should be done them, that they should not be burdened above their strength, and that none of their goods should be taken except according to law.'[5] But these pious wishes are capable of widely differing interpretations. Yahya says that he who cannot pay the poll-tax is given relief, and also he

<hr />

[1] M., 1, 81.   [2] Agh., 15, 18.   [3] Eut., 2, 434.   [4] M., 2, 203.
[5] Kh., 71.

who cannot pay the land tax.[1] But in the *Kitāb ul Umm* it is stated that if a *dhimmi* is poor the ruler is one of his creditors, and cannot spend money from the treasury on a poor *dhimmi*.[2]

Muslims did look down on the *dhimmis*, as this story shows. Ya'kūb b. Ishāk of Kinda, a Jew, was the most prominent philosopher and physician of his age and a favoured attendant of Māmūn. One day he came into the presence of the caliph and took a seat higher than that of a leading Muslim, who said, 'Why do you, a Jew, sit above the scholars of Islam?' Ya'kūb answered, 'Because I know what you know; and you do not know what I know.'[3]

Mustansir (350–366) sat in his audience hall, with the chiefs of the protected Christians in Andalus around him, among them Walīd b. Khaizurān, the *kadi* of the Christians in Cordova, and 'Ubaidulla b. Kāsim, the metropolitan of Toledo.[4] In 379 a Jew was governor of Sīrāf.[5] Another influential Jew was Ibn 'Allān, who farmed the taxes of Basra. When his wife died all Basra, except the *kadi*, followed the bier. The sultan borrowed one hundred thousand dinars from him, and he paid the same sum and one hundred horses to Khamaratakin for the taxes of Basra. Khamaratakin and Kuharain had him murdered when he was living under the protection of Nizām ul Mulk. After the murder, Nizām ul Mulk shut himself up in his house for three days, and the sultan had to cajole him into appearing in public.[6]

[1] P. 9.   [2] Umm, 4, 102.   [3] Ch.M., 55.   [4] Mak., 1, 252.
[5] Ecl., 3, 150.   [6] Ath., y. 472.

We hear of the easy circumstances and great expenditure of the Copts in their houses, while at the government office they wore the poorest clothes, ate the coarsest food, and rode on donkeys. 'At home they changed from one state to another, and passed from non-existence to existence.'[1] Mustansir gave a robe of honour to Sarūr ul Jallāl, who restored the Church of George in Cairo.[2] Christians took some part in the social life of the Muslims. At Ishna, at weddings and other rejoicings of the Muslims, the Christians were present, chanted in the Sahidic dialect of Coptic, and walked before the bridegroom through the bazaars and streets. This was a recognized custom, and continued to the time of the writer.[3]

The Muslims did not hold entirely aloof from the protected religions. A building in Bethlehem was set apart as a mosque, and 'Umar made the Christians promise to provide lights in it, keep it in repair, and clean it.[4] The monasteries were often popular with the Muslims, for in many cases the situation made them pleasant places for picnics. To that of Kusair the people of Cairo went from time to time to refresh themselves. That of Khanāfīs, in Mesopotamia, was favoured, for it was high above the villages and looked down on the rivers and meadows. It is recorded that Saif ud Dawla seldom passed that of Mart Marūtha without stopping. Wine, the forbidden, was one of the attractions. In the convent of the Virgins were taverns. The poets tell that wine and women were among the charms.

'How often have I been awakened in the dark

[1] Subh., 4, 43.   [2] A.S., 88.   [3] A.S., 278.   [4] Y.

night for my morning draught by the voices of the monks reciting the prayers loudly, clad in black, girt about the waist with the *zunnār*, with crowns of hair on their heads.' Ibn ul Mu'tazz. († 296.)[1]

'When I have completed a full year, go with me to the vineyards of Awāna, and find me a drinking place in the monastery at 'Alth; perchance I shall make friends with the monks. Fair girls reading a book of the gospel attend mass in the morning. They wear skins, but God made them slender underneath; shamefaced till the cup goes round, when they discover throat and body.' Jahza ul Barmaki. († 326.)[2]

'Drink to the sound of the *nākūs*', says another poet.

Sometimes Muslims ill repaid the hospitality of the monasteries. Some men took refuge in the Convent of the Virgins, and, when the danger was past, they bound the priest and violated the nuns.[3] During the disturbances that accompanied the fall of the Umayyads, a band of freebooters attacked a nunnery in Egypt. One of the nuns was a remarkably beautiful girl, who had taken the vows at the age of three. The men wondered what to do with her, whether to cast lots for her or to take her to the caliph. She told them that she had inherited from her soldier forefathers an ointment that made a man invulnerable, 'against him iron became as wax'. She offered them to let them make trial of it on her, and if she spoke the truth they were to let her go. She anointed herself with holy oil, knelt down, and told the strongest man with the sharpest sword to

[1] Y., 2, 678; cf. I.H., 140; Agh., 8, 178.   [2] Y., 2, 681.   [3] Y.

strike. He struck, and cut off her head. Then they understood what had been in her mind, left the other nuns, and went away praising God. Makrīzi tells much the same story, but without the last two words.[1]

Some monasteries were rich; Mar Sim'ān, near Damascus, is said to have had a revenue of four hundred thousand dinars.[2]

Pleasure was not the only object in visiting these places. In the monastery of Mīmās, between Damascus and Hims, the saint was reputed to heal the sick. The poet Batīn was ill, so he was brought to the saint to be cured. He thought that the monks neglected him, so he micturated before the tomb of the saint. Later he chanced to die and it was reported that the saint had killed him. The populace went to destroy the monastery, saying, 'Shall a Christian kill a Muslim? We will not be satisfied unless you give us the bones of the saint to burn.' A Christian bribed the governor of Hims to drive away the crowd. Excursions were also made to a place beside the monastery of Barsūma, near Malatia. Here even Muslims used to make vows. Yākūt tells of a merchant who paid such a vow after a successful business journey. The monastery paid ten thousand dinars yearly to the emperor from the proceeds of these vows.[3] Benjamin of Tudela says that the chiefs of the Muslims prayed at the tomb of Ezekiel because of the love they bore him.[4] He also says that the tomb of Daniel was in Khuzistan, in a town that was divided into two parts by a river. Each half of the

[1] S., 185 ; M., 2, 493.   [2] Y.   [3] Y.   [4] Benj., 63.

town was anxious to keep the body of the prophet, so it stayed for a year in each half alternately. Both Jews and Muslims accompanied it when it was carried over the river from one side to the other.[1]

Sometimes Christians obtained great influence; due in part to force of character, and in part perhaps to superstition. When the boat in which Mar Kuriakos was travelling arrived at the castle of the Hebrews, and passed along the side of it which faces the east, the believers of Mosul sent and stopped it in its course, giving the owner of the boat much money to stop it, and crowds upon crowds of Christians and Arabs came forth to see that blessed man and to be blessed by him (c. 136).[2] In Egypt, when the patriarch Michael anointed with oil the lunatic daughter of an official named 'Isā, and prayed over her, the devil left her.[3] The wife of Mansūr bore a child in response to the prayers of the bishop Isaac—at least, so the Christians said—so when Mansūr became caliph he made him patriarch.[4]

When the danger of a low Nile had been removed by the prayers of the Christians, Abū 'Aun did good to them and their churches and made the *kharāj* lighter.[5] When Ahmad b. Tūlūn was dying he ordered the people to pray for him. They prayed in the mosque of Mahmūd, on the flank of Mukattam, and the Jews and Christians were there also, standing apart from the Muslims. They did the same on the next day, when women and children were present, and continued doing so till he died.[6] When Timur-

---

[1] Benj., 70.   [2] Thomas, 1, 246.   [3] S., 179.   [4] S., 205.
[5] S., 200.   [6] K., 231.

tash, the Ortokid lord of Mardīn, was ill and the doctors could not help him, he had recourse to the prayers of the Christians, and sent to the convent of Mar Barsama for the right hand of the saint. He saw a man shining in light, who said to him, ' The Christians have sent me to take you from death.' He was healed on the spot. He did much to make the lot of the Christians easier and granted favours to the churches of Nisibis, Mardīn, Mayafārekīn, Ras 'Ain, Dāra, and other places in his dominion.[1]

Non-Muslim birth never prevented a man from winning a high religious position among the Muslims. To take two examples : Ma'rūf of Karkh, who died in 200, an ascetic and worker of wonders, was the son of a Christian,[2] and Hasan b. 'Abdulla b. al Marzabān Sairafi, the *kadi*, was the son of a Magian. He died in 368.[3]

In one respect some Christians had a bad reputation. Ahmad b. 'Ali Rāzi ' was even dirtier than the monks '.[4]

Once, at any rate, Christians preferred Muslim rule to Christian.

Philardus, an Armenian in the pay of Constantinople (Ibn ul Athīr calls him Firdaus), captured Antioch from the Muslims, appointed a Persian named Ismail governor, and marched away. When Sulaimān, the son of that Kutulmish who was killed near Constantinople, heard that Philardus had gone, he prepared ships, for he had just conquered Antartus and Tarsus, and attacked Antioch from the side of the hills, the Persian governor helping

[1] Lang., 312.   [2] Abu l Fida, y. 200.   [3] A.M., II, 2, 23.
[4] A.M., II, 2, 28.

him. He captured the Church of Kusyān, and seized all the furniture, and vessels of gold and silver, and the deposits of the townsmen, a great sum. He turned the church into a mosque. He proclaimed peace in the town, stopped the slaughter, prevented the Turks from entering the houses of the Christians, and from taking their daughters even for marriage. He did not let them remove from Antioch any of the plunder of the town, but made them sell it there at cheap rates. He pleased the townsmen, and the governor surrendered to him the citadel. The inhabitants preferred him to Philardus, who was nominally a Christian. This capture of Antioch took place in 477.[1]

To insult a Muslim by calling him a Jew, Christian, Magian, or idolater was a punishable offence.[2]

---

[1] B.H., 257 f.   [2] Mud., 4, 396.

CHAPTER XI

MEDICINE AND LITERATURE

IT is well known that under the caliphs many of the physicians were Jews or Christians. It is not the purpose of this book to give a detailed history of them and what they did; that belongs to the history of science. Our concern is with their relations to their rulers and fellow subjects.[1]

A historian says that in the reign of Mu'āwia many people died of poison, and goes on to tell in detail how Ibn Uthāl, a Christian physician, poisoned 'Abd ur Rahmān b. Khālid at the order of the caliph, leaving his readers to draw their own conclusions. Another Christian, Abu l Hakam, attended Yazīd as doctor when he led the pilgrimage.[2]

Khasīb, a native of Basra, was summoned to treat the governor of the town, who was the son of the caliph, as Saffāh. The patient died, so the doctor was arrested on suspicion and put in prison, where he died.[3]

Jurjis b. Bukhtishu' lived at Jundeshāpūr, where he worked in a hospital, which he seems to have regarded as his private property. The caliph Mansūr fell ill, and, as none of the Baghdad doctors could cure him, he sent for Jurjis. When he came into the presence, he offered prayers for the caliph in both Persian and Arabic in very polished langu-

[1] Facts in this section are from Tabak., unless other references are given.
[2] Agh., 15, 13.   [3] Agh., 13, 95.

age, so that the caliph was surprised and made him
sit. Some time after the caliph noticed that Jurjis'
health was suffering. Thinking that this was due
to the lack of wine, which he was accustomed to
drink, he had some brought from Kutrubbul for
him. On a Christmas Day Jurjis had an audience
with Mansūr, who asked him, 'What do you eat?'
He said, 'All good things, as the Lord pleases.'
The caliph said, 'I hear that you have no wife.'
He replied, 'I have an old bedridden wife.' The
caliph waited till he had gone, and ordered Sālim,
the chief eunuch, to choose three beautiful Greek
slave girls and take them to the physician, with
three thousand dinars. Jurjis was not at his house
when they arrived, but when he came home he said to
his pupil, 'Servant of Satan, why did you let them
into my house? Do you wish to defile me?' He
called the eunuch, and sent the girls with him back to
the caliph. When Mansūr heard this, he asked him
why he had sent the girls back. He answered, 'We
Christians do not have more than one wife. So long
as one of us has a wife living, our law forbids him to
take another.' This pleased the caliph, so he gave
orders that the physician should go in to his wives
and concubines without hindrance. He gave him
increased honour and loved him as himself.[1] It is
said of Bukhtishu' b. Jibrail also, that the caliphs
trusted him to visit their concubines.[2] Rashīd called
in Māsaweih to attend his sister. The doctor insisted on seeing the patient, and was allowed to see and
touch her in the presence of her brother. Naturally
these men often had great influence. Rashīd said of

---

[1] Cf. B.H., 125.   [2] Fih., 296.

Jibrail b. Bukhtishu', 'Let all who have petitions to bring to me speak to Jibrail, for I answer every request and fulfil every desire which he brings to me.' Sometimes they abused their position. 'Isā b. Shahlā followed Jurjis b. Bukhtishu' in the service of Mansūr. He stretched out his hand against the metropolitans and bishops, to take their wealth for himself. He even wrote to the metropolitan of Nisibis, asking for some of the church vessels, which were worth a big sum, threatening him if he delayed. In his letter were the words, 'Do you not know that the kingdom is in my hand? If I choose I make it sick, and if I choose I make it well.' The metropolitan contrived to put the letter in the hands of the vizier, who gave it to the caliph. He confiscated the property of 'Isā and banished him.[1] A new doctor might expect to have his knowledge tested or to have tricks played on him. When Bukhtishu' b. Jibrail first came to Baghdad, the caliph sent to him the water of an ox, and told him it was the water of one of his wives. The doctor was not deceived.

Jibrail b. Bukhtishu' was also famous as a doctor, and served Rashīd. A girl whom the caliph loved suffered from a stiff arm, and the physicians exhausted themselves in preparing ointments and modes of treatment, but did her no good. Rashīd summoned Jibrail and told him what had happened. He said, ' I can treat her if you will bring her into the audience hall before the whole court. I will do what seems good to me; only be not hasty and

[1] Tabak., 1, 125. The father's name is also given as Shulāfa.

angry.' The caliph agreed and sent for her. As soon as he saw her, Jibrail ran to her and took hold of her trousers, as if he wished to uncover her nakedness. From excess of shame the girl grew hot and sweated, her limbs relaxed, she moved the stiff arm, and took hold of her trousers, shielding herself. Jibrail left her instantly, and said to the caliph, 'Now she is cured.' The girl moved her arm to right and left, to the amazement of the caliph and all who were present.

His salary was twelve thousand dirhams monthly. Māmūn imprisoned him and confiscated his goods, because he had tended Amīn, but later restored him to favour and gave to him more than had been taken from him. In the time of Rashīd, a salary of a thousand dirhams monthly, with an allowance of twenty thousand a year and provisions, was paid to Māsaweih. Jibrail received ten thousand a month, an allowance of a hundred thousand a year, besides regular gifts and estates.

Muslim writers are generous in recognizing the merit of these men who did not follow their religion. Hunain, who lived in the time of Māmūn, is called the leader of his day in medicine. Hibatulla b. Tilmīdh was 'the Hippocrates of his age and the Galen of his day'. Ibn Khallikān wonders that a man of his intelligence did not accept Islam. His contemporary, Abu l Barakāt Hibatulla, the Jew, was called the 'solitaire of the age'.

Even Mutawakkil could not dispense with these sectarian doctors. Hunain wore the *zunnār*. Bukhtishu' b. Jibrail stood high in the caliph's favour, so much so that he had the same clothes, respect,

wealth, horses, slaves, and slave girls as he had.
One day, as the doctor sat beside the caliph wearing
a robe of Greek atlas, Mutawakkil noticed that the
robe was slightly torn. He kept him in talk, and
made the tear bigger till it reached the sleeve. The
doctor, however, saw what he was doing. The talk
was of mad men, and the caliph asked, ' When do
you admit that a mad man needs chains ? ' The
answer was, ' When the mad man tears the garment
of his doctor to the sleeve, then we know that he
needs chains.' The caliph laughed till he fell on his
side. Nevertheless, the caliph came to envy him,
and confiscated all his goods. It is said that he had
him flogged, one hundred and fifty lashes, laid in
fetters and imprisoned. Another story is that
Bukhtishu' was banished to Bahrain.[1]

The account of an entertainment given by him to
Mutawakkil is in the best style of the *Arabian
Nights*. He brought up all the thermantidotes
(screens that were wetted to cool the air) in the
capital, so that every place in his house where the
caliph could pass might be cool. He used to sit in
an ebony carriage, and came from the palace with a
thousand men in attendance. From evening till
midnight he indulged in all manner of orgies, then
he rose to pray, surrounded by black eunuchs, of
whom he was fond. After prayer he sat down to
conversation, read the gospel till morning, and then
went to the palace. He disobeyed the law of the
church, and took two wives at once. It is said that
every night he spent five hundred dinars on candles,
ointments, and perfumes. When all was taken from

<hr>

[1] T., III, 1437, 1447

him, the wood, coal, and wine in his house were sold for six thousand dinars. The purchaser sold it again for twelve thousand.[1]

When Salāmaweih was ill, Mu'tasim sent his son to visit him, and when he died had the funeral service celebrated in the palace, with candles and incense in his presence, after the manner of the Christians. The caliph also fasted for a day.

Sinān, the Sabian, was appointed by Muktadir to examine all who wished to practise medicine, and without his leave none could act as doctors. One day an elegantly dressed old doctor came to him. Sinān rose and went forward to greet him. When he wished to examine him and find out what was the matter, the old man pulled out a purse, holding a large sum in gold, and said, ' Sir, believe me, I cannot write my name and have not studied, but I have a big family, and they live by my practice. I beseech you, do not take from me the bread that God gives.' Sinān laughed, and told him that he would permit him to practise if he would agree not to approach dangerous cases, not to open an artery, and not to use purgatives. The old man promised to use only oxymel, and drugs like it. The next day a fashionable young doctor came to him, and Sinān asked under whom he had studied. He replied, 'Under my father, who came to you yesterday.' Sinān laughed, and imposed on him the same conditions as on the father.[2]

Hibatulla b. Tilmīdh was very grave, and in all his intercourse with Muktafi was only once known to make a joke. A sinecure in the ' House of

[1] B.H., 157.　　　[2] B.H., 175.

Bottles' had been taken from him by the vizier, without the caliph's knowledge. At the end of a visit the old man found great difficulty in standing up, so the caliph asked what was the matter. 'My bottles are broken.' Now this was a slang phrase, used in Baghdad, to denote old age. Muktafi was so struck at this piece of slang on the lips of the dignified old gentleman that he made enquiries and restored to him his sinecure. When he died, in 560, the whole of Baghdad attended the funeral.[1]

The physicians sometimes suffered through palace intrigues. The famous doctor and excellent physician Amīn ud Dawla Abu l Karam Sā'id b. Toma, a Jacobite of Baghdad, was killed on Thursday, 28 Jumādā 1, 618. He was skilled in healing, trustworthy in his deeds, wise, generous, a good mediator in supplying the needs of the poor, answering their requests, and visiting them. The caliph Nāsir loved, respected, and honoured him, and entrusted to him the treatment of his kingdom, his sons, his daughters, and his wives. At the end of his life the caliph's eyes grew weak, so that he could not see to write confidential letters to the vizier. He found a woman in Baghdad, named Sitt Nasīm, whose writing could not be distinguished from that of the caliph. He took her into the palace, told her his secrets, and whenever he wanted to write she wrote at his dictation. The vizier thought that her letters were in the caliph's own hand, for he concealed his blindness. This lasted some time. Then a certain eunuch, Tāj ud Dīn Rashīk, made an agreement with her, and they wrote what they chose when the

[1] I. Khall.

caliph dictated, and their orders were carried out. One day the vizier, Muayyid ud Dīn, wrote to the caliph, and received a confused and disordered reply, and therefore felt doubtful about it, and made secret enquiry from Amīn ud Dawla. He told him of the caliph's blindness, of the woman whose writing was like his, of the eunuch Rashīk who was in league with her, and the letters they wrote as they chose without the caliph's knowledge. The vizier began to disregard the orders sent him. The woman and eunuch were angry with Amīn ud Dawla for betraying them, because he was the only one to meet and speak with the vizier who knew their secret. They suborned two brothers, the sons of Kamar ud Dīn, who lay in wait for the doctor one night as he left the palace to go to his house, sprang on him, and stabbed him twice with daggers. When he saw them, he cried out, ' Seize them, they are so and so.' These evil men heard him, came back and finished him, and wounded also the servant with him who carried the lantern. The city and palace were roused, and the dead man was carried to his house and buried there. Nine months later they took him to the Church of Mar Thomas, and buried him with his fathers. On the night in which he was killed, those two wicked murderers were taken, disembowelled, and impaled on the spot where they had killed him.[1]

It was not only the Muslims who travelled. Ya'kūb b. Saklān, of Jerusalem, who died in 626, was doctor to al 'Adil b. Ayyūb. Later he was taken to Damascus, where he prospered. Towards

[1] B.H., 449 f.

the end of his life he was crippled by gout, so al Malik
ul Mu'azzam sent a litter to fetch him when he
needed his professional attentions.[1] About the year
570, two Jews, Jehūda and his son Samuel, migrated
from the west. Samuel went to Adherbaijān, and
became physician to the house of Pahlawān. Afterwards he turned Muslim.[2] Yūsuf b. Yahya b. Ishāk,
of Fez, fled from his home when 'Abd ul Mumin
persecuted the Jews and Christians, went to Egypt,
and then to Aleppo. From there he travelled in
Irak and India. On his return he had a big practice
and was a close friend of al Kifti, the author of the
History of Learned Men. He died a Jew in 623.[3]

Yuhannā b. Māsaweih served the caliphs from
Rashīd to Mutawakkil, and was always present at
their meal times. He was enough of a favourite
with Mutawakkil to be allowed to chaff him mildly.
He could also make jokes at the expense of Islam,
jokes recorded by Muslim writers. To a priest who
suffered from indigestion, and had tried all the
remedies the doctor could recommend, he said,
'Turn Muslim; this is good for the digestion.'
When 'Isā b. Ibrāhīm b. Nūh, the secretary of al
Fath b. 1 Khākān turned Muslim, Yuhannā came
home from the palace to find some monks in his
house, and said to them, 'Get out of my house,
children of sin. Turn Muslim, for the Messiah has
just turned Muslim.'

In spite of the wealth and influence which these
men attained, Muslims felt that they belonged to a
lower class. This comes out very clearly in the
following incident. Under orders from the vizier,

[1] B.H. Mu., 443.   [2] B.H. Mu., 377.   [3] Kifti, 392.

Sinān b. Thābit sent a travelling dispensary round Irak. The doctors found that Sūra and Nahr Malik were inhabited mainly by Jews, so asked whether they should work there or go to some place where the people were Muslims. Sinān knew that the hospitals in Baghdad treated both Muslims and *dhimmis*, but asked for instructions from the vizier, who sent this order : ' We agree that the treatment of *dhimmis* and animals is right, but men must be treated before animals, and Muslims before *dhimmis*. If anything is left over which Muslims do not need, let it be used on the class below them.'[1]

It may be mentioned that Bukhtishu' b. Jibrail endowed the monastery where his father was buried.[2]

Doctors sometimes quarrelled. Jurjis, who was named the Philosopher on the same principle that the crow is called Father of Whiteness, wrote verses on Salāma b. Rahmūn, the Jew :

> What is good weighs light in the scales of Abu l Khair, for he is ignorant.
>
> By his bad luck his poor patient is in a shoreless ocean of death.
>
> To him come three at once—the doctor's face, the bier, and the washer of the dead.[3]

LITERATURE

During the first and second centuries relations between the Arabs and their subjects in the sphere of letters and arts were very friendly, and even in later times much of the old friendliness endured. It has been pointed out elsewhere that the government employed non-Muslims as engineers and architects. One may add here that Kuseir

---

[1] Kifti, 194.   [2] Kifti, 142.   [3] B.H. Mu., 348.

'Amra, a hunting lodge of an Umayyad prince,
was decorated by painters who knew no Arabic.
Religion made no difference to the treatment of
poets and musicians by the great. Hunain, the
Christian singer of Hīra, was an intimate friend of
Bishr b. Marwān, and an article of six pages is
devoted to him in the *Kitāb ul Aghāni*.[1] Barsauma,
the flute player, often performed before Hārūn
Rashīd. As he is called a Nabataean and his name
is Aramaic, it is almost certain that he was a
Christian.[2] The poet Abū Zubaid was treated with
courtesy by 'Uthmān,[3] verses by the Jewish poet
Abū Zannād were set to music by Ibn Mashaj abū
'Uthmān Sa'īd.[4]

In the whole of Arabic literature there is only
one *dhimmi* who has a great reputation among
Muslims, and he is the poet al Akhtal. He with
Sarjūn and Kāsim b. Tawīl ul 'Ibādi were companions of Yazīd in his amusements.[5] Al Akhtal
was respected as a judge of poetry, though he was
once accused of accepting a jar of wine as a bribe.[6]
When he went to Kūfa, Sha'bi visited him to listen
to his poetry, and was invited to dine and drink
wine with him.[7] It was he who said, ' When a
connoisseur in poetry hears a fine verse, he does not
care whether the author is Muslim or Christian ; '
and the sentiment was often true, though Hammād
ur Rāwi could say, ' I will not speak of the verse of
a man who made Christian poetry popular.'[8] The
caliph Hārūn declared that the highest and most

---

[1] Agh., 2, 116.   [2] Agh., 6, 72.   [3] Agh., 11, 23.
[4] Agh., 19, 102.   [5] Agh., 6, 128. 16, 68.   [6] Agh., 7, 40.
[7] Agh., 8, 81.   [8] Agh., 7, 165, 172.

fulsome (*afkhar*) praise ever sung of a caliph was
the line by al Akhtal: 'Till they are brought to him,
the sun of enmity, most clement when they are
overcome.'[1]

Mu'āwia, or, in another version of the story, his
son Yazīd, had no scruple in employing al Akhtal
to lampoon the inhabitants of Medina, who had
angered him, when other poets refused to attack
them, on the religious ground that they could not
lampoon those who had sheltered and helped the
Prophet.[2] For this freedom he narrowly escaped
having his tongue torn out.

Jarīr recited to 'Abd ul Malik a poem in praise of
Hajjāj, and when it was finished the caliph told al
Akhtal to praise the Commander of the Faithful.
He stood opposite and recited a poem, most poetical
and most fulsome. The caliph said, 'You are our
poet and our panegyrist; ride on him.' He made
ready to do so, but Jarīr said, 'Commander of the
Faithful, a Christian unbeliever should not be above
a Muslim, should not overpower him, nor ride on
him.' The courtiers supported him, so the caliph
told al Akhtal to stop.[3] The same feeling of the
superiority of Islam comes out in the answer of
Jarīr to the question whether he or al Akhtal was
the better poet; 'I was helped against him by the
burden of his age and his lack of the true religion;
still I never saw him without fearing that he would
swallow me.'[4] One writer points out that his rivals
Farazdak and Jarīr belonged to Mudar, and so, as a
matter of course, Rabī'a took the side of al Akhtal

[1] Agh., 10, 4.   [2] Agh., 13, 147.
[3] Amali, 3, 43.   [4] Muwashshah, 130.

and upheld his claim to be a great poet.[1] Religious
jealousy may lie behind this statement, an attempt
to belittle the Christian by suggesting that tribal
pride and not merit gave him his reputation.
Except for a few verses which will be noticed later,
there is practically nothing in his poetry to distinguish it from the compositions of Muslim poets.

The covenant of 'Umar says that *dhimmis* are
not to learn the Koran or teach it to their children.
In 235 Mutawakkil forbade Muslims to teach Christians.[2] There was some prejudice against teaching
the Koran to non-Muslims. Certain *dhimmis* asked
Abū 'Uthmān al Māzini to read with them the
book, the grammar of Sībawaih, offering him a
hundred dinars for his trouble. Although he was
poor he refused. When a friend remonstrated with
him he said, ' In the book are three hundred traditions and ever so many verses of the Koran ; I will
not give a *dhimmi* such mastery over our religion.'
Shortly after he was summoned into the presence
of the caliph al Wāthik to explain a point of grammar, and was given a thousand dinars. His comment
was, ' I gave God one hundred dinars and He has
given me one thousand.' In this anecdote there is
no hint that the teaching of the Koran to *dhimmis*
had ever been forbidden by law; the objection is
simply a matter of conscience. Indeed, the law of
Mutawakkil remained a dead letter, and famous
dhimmis studied under Muslim teachers.[3]

Hunain b. Ishāk studied under Khalīl b. Ahmad
and Sībawaih, and became a master of Arabic.[4]

---

[1] Muwashshah, 138.   [2] M., 2, 494.
[3] Agh., 8, 136 n.   [4] Tabak., 1, 185, 189.

Yahya b. 'Adi b. Hamīd became the chief logician of his day, and was a pupil of al Fārabi.[1] Thābit b. Kurra was a pupil of Muhammad b. Mūsā, who introduced him to Mu'tadid.[2] Ibn Jazla studied under 'Ali b. Walīd, a Mutazelite; he wrote a beautiful hand and was a scholar of literature. His books reveal his quality and his knowledge. He afterwards turned Muslim.[3] He died in 493. It may not be amiss to mention that the same tolerance was sometimes found among Christians; Mattai b. Yūnus, a Nestorian, studied under Jacobite teachers.[4]

Ibrāhīm b. Hilāl may be taken as an example of what a *dhimmi* might become. He held high office, poets praised him, and Bakhtiyār, the Buwayhid, offered him the post of vizier if he would turn Muslim; but he refused. His relations with Muslims were good. He exchanged letters, gifts and presents with the Sahib Ismail b. 'Abbād and also with the sharīf ar Rida; though religion separated them, letters united them. He knew the Koran. He used to tell this story of the death of his father, Hilāl. 'The vizier al Muhallabi paid me a visit of condolence. When I knew that he was on the way to my house, I went out to meet him and begged him not to take the trouble to come inside. He would not listen, but came up and sat for a time, saying everything that would encourage the mind and comfort the heart. He praised and lauded my father, and said, "That man is not dead who has you as his heir and substitute."' When Ibrāhīm died, the sharīf ar Rida wrote an elegy upon him. Some murmured

[1] B.H. Mu., 296. [2] B.H. Mu., 265.
[3] Tabak., 1, 255; I. Khall., 3, 256. [4] B.H. Mu., 285.

that a sharīf should lament a Sabian. Ar Rida
defended himself on the ground that he lamented
only the excellence that was in the man. It is said
that his letters, both official and private, were among
the most finished that were written at that time.
Yākūt devotes thirty-four pages to him in his
Dictionary of Learned Men.[1]

In 385 Bishr b. Hārūn, a Christian, died. He
had been a secretary and a poet, a lampoonist with
a sharp tongue.[2] Though there was prejudice against
Christians and others, yet it cannot have been very
strong or general if an historian thought it worth
while to record the death of such an inconspicuous
man as this.

The account of al Akhtal given by ibn Rashīk is
very different in temper from that in the *Kitāb ul
Aghāni*, and shows religion turning into fanaticism.

'Al Akhtal was one of the great poets of the
second period, and by virtue of his poetry became
a companion of 'Abd ul Malik, who made him ride
on the back of Jarīr, a pious Muslim. It is said that
the reason for this order was a poetical contest in
his presence. The poet, the curse of God be on
him, openly attacked Islam and belittled the Muslims. He said: "I do not fast obediently in Ramadān,
I do not eat the flesh of sacrifices; I do not drive
strong young camels to the valley of Mecca to get
success; I do not cry at night, like others, 'Come
to salvation.' But I will drink cold wine and worship before the break of dawn."

'Religious toleration was very advanced when
kings could listen to words like this! But for his

[1] Y.Ir., 1, 324; A.M., II, 2, 54.   [2] A.M., II, 2, 59.

poetry, he would have been killed for his lampoons on the Ansar; and his abusive reply to Jarīr would have ruined a descendant of 'Ali, let alone a Christian.'[1]

These words show an entirely new spirit, for there is a fierceness in them that has not been seen earlier. The isolation produced by spiritual pride has given the writer swelled head (this is a good Arabic idiom) and destroyed his sense of humour. Otherwise, he would have seen the absurdity of calling these innocent words an attack on Islam. The mental segregation and consequent decay of Islam has begun.

Muslim philosophy and science began in translations. Many, if not most, of those who turned books from Greek and Syriac into Arabic were Christians. One of the earliest of them, Stephen the elder, worked for Khālid, the grandson of Mu'āwia.[2] The caliphs Mansūr and Māmūn especially employed men on this work. It is said that the three sons of Mūsā, famous patrons of learning, paid five hundred dinars monthly for translation work.[3]

It would be hard to overestimate the importance of men like Hunain b. Ishāk and Thābit b. Kurra, but their work was not literature. The philologists and grammarians despised them. Yākūt has recorded a discussion, between Abū Sa'īd Hasan b. 'Abdulla us Sīrāfi and Mattai b. Yūnus, wherein Hasan speaks of 'men, weak and imperfect in one tongue, who translate it into another, in which they are also weak and imperfect'.[4] The whole discussion shows the Arab belief in the unique value of his language. Nevertheless, bibliographers and

¹ Umda, 1, 21.   ² Fih., 244.   ³ Fih., 243.   ⁴ Y.Ir., 3, 117.

historians have preserved the names of these men, in spite of the defects of their Arabic.

When Mukhtār, who was called Ibn Batlān († 455), quarrelled with Ibn Ridwān, he wrote a letter attacking him, pointing out his faults and calling attention to his ignorance.[1] In this case, at any rate, a Christian carried on a controversy with a Muslim on an equal footing with his opponent.

Ibn Khallikān thought the poetry of Hibatulla b. Tilmīdh worth quoting, though Yākūt criticizes it as not being as good as his prose. Makkari thought Ismail the Jew and his daughter Kasmūna deserving of mention as poets.[2] In Spain, too, Mansūr, the Jewish singer, was sent as a representative of the caliph with Ziryāb, the Persian musician.[3]

Though Muslim scholars often show a great lack of curiosity about those things that do not belong to Islam, yet there are brilliant exceptions. Al Birūni's book on India stands alone; in it he treats of the land and people, their habits, religion, and philosophy. Ibn Hazm, of Spain († 456), had a very good knowledge of the Bible and Christian theology. Ibn Khaldūn knew the outer form of the Bible and something about the organization of the church, and fitted these things into the *Prolegomena* to the study of history. One subject that drew interest was the calendar. Al Birūni dealt exhaustively with the various systems of counting time in the *Kānūn Mas'ūdi*. Kalkashandi thought a knowledge of the religious festivals of the *dhimmis* necessary to a secretary. He is well acquainted with the feasts, the stories connected with, and the customs observed

[1] B.H. Mu., 331.   [2] Mak., 2, 236.   [3] Mak., 2, 85.

at them; he knows, for example, of the searching of
the house for leaven before the Passover. In speaking of such things, he does permit himself at times
a pious sniff. Makrīzi gives even more detail about
Christian and Jewish festivals, describes the various
sects, gives a list of the patriarchs of Alexandria as
an essential part of the history of Egypt, and says
something about the history of Christianity and
Judaism. Kazwīni describes the calendars in his
Wonders of Creation. Mas'ūdi's interests also went
beyond the bounds of Islam. In the *Kitāb ut
Tanbīh* he tells the legend of the translation of
the Septuagint, gives in outline the history of Constantinople with a list of the Œcumenical Councils,
a fairly accurate account of the various heresies and
sects, and the intricacies of Christian theology and
theologians.

The earlier Christians wrote either in Syriac or
Coptic, and did not appeal to a Muslim audience.
Severus b. Mukaffa' broke through literary tradi
tion and wrote Arabic as it was spoken, and
so courted the disdain of fashionable scholars.
Christians helped to preserve their separate existence by writing Arabic in Syriac or Coptic
letters. Later, Jews and Christians wrote in Arabic,
but for the most part their work lay apart from the
main stream of Arabic letters. Saadya translated the
Law into Arabic, but Muslims took no notice of it.
Makrīzi must have used books written by *dhimmis,*
but he is careful not to name the authors. Mas'ūdi
knows of books by Christians, and praises the
histories of Kais the Maronite and Eutychius of
Alexandria; also one by Abū Zakaria of Kuskar,

and another by a Jacobite, who was also named Abū Zakaria.[1] This is, however, unusual; Christian writers are generally ignored. Al Makīn and Bar Hebræus have a higher reputation in the west than in the east.

The Book of Religion and Empire, by 'Ali Tabari, with its many quotations from the Bible, stands by itself, for it is a defence of Islam by a convert from Christianity. Still it is hard to imagine that it could have been popular, except among those who knew something about the Bible.

Another unique book is the *Apology* of al Kindi, which was written shortly before 300. The author, whoever he may have been, writes with the greatest freedom and criticizes Islam severely. He finds fault with the doctrine of the sacred war, makes fun of the ceremonies of the pilgrimage, comparing Indian rites, and criticizes the mothers of the faithful—the wives of the Prophet. What is perhaps more remarkable, he quotes a speech by the caliph attacking the hypocrisy of the courtiers in religious matters.

The *kadi* of Harrān had a Syriac account of the Sabian religion translated carefully into Arabic for the benefit of 'Ali b. 'Isā.[2]

Al Asbagh, the son of 'Abd ul 'Azīz, is said to have read Christian books with the help of a deacon, to see if they contained blasphemies against Muhammad.[3]

Writers, especially the geographers, often record curious facts concerning *dhimmis*. A few examples may not be out of place. Near Safed is a cave in

---

[1] Mas.T., 154.   [2] Fih., 327.   [3] S., 134.

which water collects once a year. Jews collect on
that day, and take the water to distant places. If a
crowd gathers and makes a noise in a church in
Nazareth, a pillar in it sweats so that the sweat can
be seen.[1] In a church in Egypt, to which you go
down by some twenty steps, is a throne, and under
the throne a dead man wrapped in leather. Above
the throne is a big marble vessel, with a glass one
inside it, and in this again a piece of hollow, twisted
brass. The sacristan puts a flaxen wick in the piece
of brass, pours in oil, and lights it. Soon the glass
is filled with oil, which overflows into the marble
jar. The sacristan takes this oil, which runs
continually, fills the lamps with it, and sells the
surplus for the maintenance of himself and the
other servants of the church. A friend tested this,
and it is true. If the dead man is taken away the
oil will not flow.[2]

In one point the covenant of 'Umar was kept;
Christians were not given names of honour containing the word *dīn*, religion. Instead they were given
names like Amīn ud Dawla.

One Muslim, at least, did not disdain to use
Christian ideas for political satire. He said: 'Turn
Christian, for that is the true religion. Our age
proves it. Confess the three, may they be exalted
and glorious ; think all else vain, for it is vain.
Ya'kūb the vizier is the father, 'Azīz is the son,
and Fadl the holy spirit.'[3]

<hr>

[1] Subh., 4, 75.   [2] I.R., 81.   [3] Ath., y. 380.

CHAPTER XII

HOLY GROUND

THE accepted version of history is that, in obedience to the tradition, 'Two religions shall not remain in the land of the Arabs', 'Umar drove all Jews and Christians out of Arabia, because that was the land of Islam and Islam alone. This is an exaggeration. The *dhimmis* were never banished from Yemen, and Hamdāni mentions a village with two hundred Jewish inhabitants in the east of the peninsula.[1] *Dhimmis* were excluded from the Hedjaz, but even this was contrary to the practice of the Prophet, was opposed to the views of some of the great lawyers, and was not carried out consistently.

During the Prophet's lifetime, *dhimmis* lived in Medina, Mecca, Khaibar, Yemen, and Nejrān, and a Christian, named Mawhib, is specially mentioned as living in Mecca.[2] 'Umar did not allow adult male captives—non-Muslims—to enter Medina, but he made an exception in favour of Abū Lulua, at the request of Mughīra b. Sha'ba, as he was a skilled workman.[3] The rule that Nabataeans trading with Medina paid only five per cent instead of ten probably implies that they visited the town.[4] Abū Zūbaid, the Christian poet, certainly visited it, for 'Uthmān drew him near to him and made him sit beside him.[5]

[1] Hamdani, 152 ; Umm, 4, 100.   [2] Suli, 214 ; Umm, 4, 101.
[3] Ibn Sa'd, III, 1, 250.   [4] Umm, 4, 125 ; M., 2, 121.
[5] Agh., 11, 23.

Hunain, the Christian singer of Hīra, stayed in Medina.[1] Abu l Hakam, a Christian, accompanied Yazīd to Mecca, when he led the pilgrimage during the reign of his father, Mu'āwia.[2] 'Abd ul Malik sent a Christian engineer to build dams in Mecca to ward off floods.[3] In 87 or 88 Walīd sent eighty Greek and Coptic masons to rebuild the Prophet's mosque; it is even said that he wrote to the emperor for them.[4] In the papyri are frequent references to *dhimmi* labourers engaged in work on mosques.

According to the *Mīzān*, Abū Hanīfa permitted an unbeliever to enter the Harām, the sacred territory round Mecca, as a traveller, while the other three imāms forbade it.[5] But in the *Kitāb ul Umm* it is stated that a *dhimmi* might visit the Hedjaz, though he might not stay longer than three days. He was only there on sufferance. If such a traveller died in Mecca the body was taken outside the sacred area for burial; if he were taken ill he was carried outside at once. One who died elsewhere in the Hedjaz, was buried where he died; if he fell ill he was taken outside the province as soon as he could be moved.[6]

MOSQUES

We have already seen that Christian masons were employed in building and rebuilding mosques. It is reported that the king of Nubia sent to 'Abdulla b. Sa'd b. abī Sarh a pulpit, and with it he sent his carpenter, Victor of Dendera, to set it up in the mosque of 'Amr.[7] In early times Christians

---

[1] Agh., 2, 122. [2] Tabak., 1, 116. [3] B., 54. [4] B., 7; I.R.,69.
[5] Mizan, 2, 162. [6] Umm, 4, 100. [7] M., 2, 248.

went into the mosques freely, though sometimes objection was taken to them. Al Akhtal acted as arbitrator for the tribe of Bakr b. Wāil, apparently more than once, and performed his duties in the mosque.[1] Khālid b. Muhājir seems to have killed Ibn Uthāl in the mosque at Damascus, as he was leaving the presence of Mu'āwia.[2] An embassy from the emperor asked permission to visit the mosque in Damascus. It was granted, and they entered by the gate opposite the dome over the *mihrāb*. When they lifted their eyes to the dome the leader fell fainting, and had to be carried to his house.[3] One of the complaints against Walīd b. 'Ukba, governor of Kūfa, was that he had given a house beside the mosque to Abū Zubaid, who made a road of it to get to Walīd's house. An aggravated form of the story is, that Abū Zubaid used to spend the night with the governor and in the morning cross the mosque drunk.[4]

'Umar ordered Abū Mūsā al Ash'ari to bring his secretary to the mosque. He explained that he could not do so because the man was a Christian, and his explanation was accepted as natural.[5]

Of the lawyers, Mālik and Ahmad forbid the entry of *dhimmis* into mosques under all circumstances. Abū Hanīfa lets them enter without special permission, while Shāfe'i requires them to get permission from the recognized authority.[6]

In early times *dhimmis* seem to have taken their lawsuits to the *kadi* in the mosque. Khair b. Nu'aim was *kadi* of Egypt from 120 to 128,

[1] Agh., 7, 171.   [2] Agh., 15, 13.   [3] I.A., 1, 210.   [4] Agh., 4, 180.
[5] Ghazi, 388 ; Uyun, 1, 62.   [6] Mizan, 2, 163.

judged Muslims in the mosque and Christians at the door, after the afternoon prayer. Others had judged Christians in their houses. It is said that the first to take Christians into the mosque was Muhammad b. Masrūk, *kadi* from 177 to 184.[1] One cannot help thinking that the historian has made a mistake. Perhaps Muhammad reverted to a former custom, and, as he was well hated, everything he did was wrong. Bukām, the Christian headman of Būra in the time of Māmūn, did not go into the mosque. On Fridays he went in procession to the gate, and then left his deputy to lead the prayers.[2]

In 720 a Christian, disguised as a Muslim, went into the mosque of Zāhir, in Cairo, and tried to set it on fire, but it is not clear that it was necessary for him so to disguise himself in order to enter.[3]

BLOOD MONEY

In the desert compensation for the killing of a man could often be made by paying blood money. After their conquests the Arabs brought this custom with them, and extended it to include the *dhimmis*. What actually happened is not clear. The evidence is conflicting; tradition contradicts tradition; the legal schools differ widely; the records of fact are few.

Both Muhammad and 'Umar are said to have put Muslims to death for murdering Christians. The Prophet said, 'Whoso kills a *dhimmi* will not smell the scent of paradise, and its scent spreads a journey of forty years;' but 'Ali said, 'A Muslim must not be killed for the murder of an unbeliever.' The

---

[1] K., 351, 390.   [2] Eut., 2, 434.   [3] M., 2, 514.

balance of opinion was against the execution of a Muslim for the murder of a *dhimmi*. Of the four imāms, only Abū Hanīfa demanded it.[1] A Christian historian says that 'Umar II forbade it, but tradition says that he ordered such an execution.[2]

There is even less agreement as to the amount of the blood money. Abū Bakr, 'Umar, and 'Uthmān demanded the full amount, the same as for a Muslim; this was also the opinion of Abū Hanīfa. Mālik said that it was one-half of what was paid for a Muslim, whether for murder or manslaughter. Shāfe'i said that it was one-third. Ahmad b. Hanbal held that for murder it was the same as for a Muslim, but for manslaughter one-half or one-third. If the victim was a woman, Ahmad demanded the full sum for murder and half for manslaughter, while the others required half of what was paid for a man. For the killing of a Magian, Abū Hanīfa demanded the full blood wit, Mālik and Shāfe'i wanted eight hundred dirhams, and Ahmad demanded eight hundred for manslaughter and one thousand, six hundred for murder.[3]

Some of these differences represent regional differences of custom, but others may be due to changes in the value of money joined with legal conservatism.

In the time of the Prophet blood money is said to have been 800 dinars, or 8,000 dirhams, for a Muslim, and half this for a *dhimmi*. In the days of 'Umar it was 1,000 dinars, or 12,000 dirhams, or 100 camels, or 200 cattle, or 2,000 sheep, or 200

[1] Bukhari, 4, 119, 120 ; Umm, 7, 291.
[2] S.A., 1, 107.   [3] Rahmat, 2, 126.

costumes consisting of wrapper, cloak, shirt, and trousers, while that for a *dhimmi* remained fixed.

The third demanded by Shāfe'i was 4,000 dirhams which is one-half the blood money in the time of the Prophet. 'Umar II fixed it at 5,000 dirhams, which is half the blood money in the time of 'Umar I, if ten dirhams are reckoned to the dinar. This suggests that the blood money for a *dhimmi* was fixed at half the sum for a Muslim, and, as the imāms fixed on different sums as the full amount, so the different fractions arose.[1]

A notice in the *Kitāb ul Aghāni* introduces further complications. Mu'āwia made the Banu Makhzūm pay blood money, 12,000 dirhams, for Ibn Uthāl. Half was paid into the treasury, and the caliph kept the other half for himself. This was the custom with blood money paid for *dhimmis* till 'Umar II gave up his share. The treasury, however, still took half, i.e. 6,000 dirhams.[2] Elsewhere it is stated that Mu'āwia put half the blood money for a *dhimmi* in the treasury.[3] The only solution that can be offered is this: at first full blood money was paid and the treasury took half, for Mu'āwia made no distinction between his private purse and the public treasury. Then the government waived its rights, and the relatives still got their half. The lawyers accepted this custom, and formulated the rule that the blood money for a *dhimmi* was half that for a Muslim.

The rule that a Muslim might not be executed for murdering a *dhimmi* was not always observed. The reason why Asad ud Dīn Shirkuh and his

---

[1] Abu Daud, 4, 308.   [2] Agh., 15, 13.   [3] Umm, 7, 291.

brother, Saladin, took service with Nūr ud Dīn
Zanji was that Shirkuh had killed a Christian, who
was a friend of the emir of Tekrit, so the two
brothers fled to escape the consequences.[1] When
the doctor Amīn ud Dawla was killed, in 618, the
two murderers were executed as soon as caught, on
the spot where they had killed their victim.[2]

If a Muslim were killed in a country inhabited by
dhimmis, they had to pay the blood money if the
murderers were not known or could not be caught.[3]

Mālik held that no expiation was necessary for
the accidental killing of a *dhimmi*; the other three
held that it was necessary.[4]

The damages to be paid for killing the unborn
child of a *dhimmi* mother were one-tenth of the blood
money for the mother. But if the mother were the
wife of a Muslim, the penalty was the same as for
the child of a Muslim woman.[5]

APOSTASY

The lawyers are agreed that death is the penalty
for apostasy from Islam, for they appeal to the
tradition, ' If a man changes his religion, kill him '.
Some held that the apostate was to be killed under
any circumstances; others argued that one who
had returned to Islam, and did not persist in his
apostasy, did not deserve to be put to death.
Various stories are told to point the moral. Usāma
killed a man after he had pronounced the confession,
' There is no god but God ', and defended himself on
the ground that the man had spoken from fear only.

[1] B.H., 330.   [2] B.H., 449.   [3] I.A., 1, 179.
[4] Mizan, 2, 129.   [5] Umm, 6, 97.

The Prophet asked, 'Did you split open his heart?' Another tells that at the conquest of Tustar a Muslim joined the unbelievers, but was captured and killed. 'Umar said, 'You should have put him in prison, fed him, and asked him to repent three days; if he did not, you might then have killed him.' Abū Mūsā kept a Jew apostate from Islam for two months, though Mu'ādh would have put him to death on the spot.[1]

The imāms agree that death is the penalty; they differ about the time when it should be inflicted. Abū Hanīfa says that it must follow immediately on sentence, though some of his school allow a delay of three days. Mālik says that the apostate must be invited to repent, and, in case of a first refusal, be given three days' grace. Two views are current under Ahmad's name. One agrees with Mālik's teaching; the other is that there is no need to invite the apostate to repent. Shāfe'i holds that he must be invited to repent, but there is no delay in carrying out sentence if he is obdurate. If the apostate is a woman, Abū Hanīfa holds that she is to be imprisoned and not executed; the others hold that she is to be treated as a man.[2]

If an apostate escaped to a foreign country he was treated as dead; his property was divided among his heirs, his slaves set free, and his wife could marry again. Anything taken from him after his arrival in a foreign land was booty.[3]

Shāfe'i ruled that if a *dhimmi* changed from one protected religion he was to be banished, for tribute

[1] Kh., 109 f.   [2] Mizan, 2, 131.   [3] Kh., 111.

is not to be taken from a man for a faith other than that for which it was taken from him at first.[1]

The opinions of the imāms do not reflect the practice of early Islam. It is said that 'Amr put this problem to 'Umar. A man turned Muslim, then apostatized, then repeated this process several times. Was his conversion to be accepted? 'Umar wrote, 'Accept it from him. Offer him Islam; if he accept, leave him alone; if not, cut off his head.'[2] Salt b. 1 'As was flogged for drunkenness by 'Umar II, when he was governor of the Hedjaz, so he turned Christian, and fled to Constantinople. An ambassador, sent to arrange an exchange of prisoners, found him there, and tried to persuade him to revert to his original faith and return to Arabia. He refused because he, his wife, and his children would be jeeringly called Christians. Another part of the story implies that he had been forced to turn Christian after his arrival in Constantinople. There is no hint that he would have been in any danger for his perversion.[3]

A Jew turned Muslim and then reverted. 'Umar II gave this command about him: 'Invite him to accept Islam; if he does, let him go. If he refuses, fetch a plank and make him lie on it, then invite him; if he still refuses, tie him to it, put a spear at his heart, and then ask him. If he returns to Islam, let him go; if he refuses, then kill him.'[4]

Frightened at the threats of Māmūn, some of the pagans of Harrān turned Muslim, but after the caliph's death many of them reverted.[5]

---

[1] Umm, 4, 105.　　[2] Hakam, 168.　　[3] Agh., 5, 175.
[4] Kh., 112.　　[5] Fih., 320.

About the year 375, complaint was made to Muhammad b. Nu'mān that a Christian, more than eighty years old, had turned Muslim and then apostatized. He was called on to repent but refused, so his case was sent to the caliph al 'Azīz. He handed him over to the chief of the police, and required the *kadi* to send four witnesses to ask him to repent. He was promised one hundred dinars if he repented, and if obstinate he was to be put to death. As he refused he was executed, and his body was thrown into the Nile.[1]

During the persecution under al Hākim, in Egypt, many *dhimmis* embraced Islam. Then the caliph changed his policy. It is even said that he was sorry for what he had done, and he gave orders that those who had apostatized might return to their former faith. One version is that some Jews and Christians came to him and said that they preferred their old faiths; he replied, ' Do what seems good to you.' His successor, az Zāhir, allowed those who had been forced to embrace Islam under al Hākim to return to their old religions, and many did so in 418.[2]

It is said that during the persecution of 'Abd ul Mumin, Maimonides was forced to pretend to be a Muslim. As soon as he could he escaped from Spain and went to Egypt, where he settled among the Jews in Old Cairo. The *kadi*, 'Abd ur Rahīm b. 'Ali al Baisāni, befriended him. A man who had known him in Spain came to Egypt and tried to injure him for his reversion to Jewry, but the *kadi* protected him.

---

[1] K., 593.   [2] B.H., 205; A.M., II, 2, 69; M., 1, 355.

A kindly tolerance was expressed in the words, 'A forced convert is not a true Muslim.'[1]

SOLDIERS

In early days, the rule in the covenant of 'Umar forbidding *dhimmis* to bear arms was unknown. The Christian poet, Abū Zubaid, fought at the battle of the bridge on the Muslim side. The historian says that he had gone to Hīra on private business, and implies that, finding himself in the neighbourhood of a fight, he naturally joined in.[2]

John of Nikiou says that 'Amr compelled the inhabitants of Egypt to fight against the Pentapolis.[3] A Christian Arab was in the army of Walīd b. 'Ukba when he raided Asia Minor.[4] In the treaty which Surāka made in 22 with Armenia, it was stipulated that they might join the Muslim army instead of paying tribute, and the wording suggests that it was expected that they would prefer military service.[5] The Jarājima of Syria fought in the Muslim ranks.[6] Marwān b. Hakam enrolled two hundred men of Aila, who were probably Christians, as police to keep order in Medina.[7] In the papyri several soldiers with Greek or Coptic names are mentioned ; as all the Muslims in these documents bear Arabic names it may be presumed that these men were Christians.[8] The Christian tribe of Taghlib carried arms and carried on a war with their neighbours, in which al Akhtal narrowly escaped death.[9] While Hafs was governor of Egypt,

[1] B.H. Mu., 417. [2] B., 252. [3] J.N., 376.
[4] Agh., 4, 183. [5] T.I. 2665. [6] B., 159.
[7] Agh., 4, 155. [8] B.M., 4, 1448, 1449. [9] Agh., 20, 126 f.

many of the natives were enrolled and became soldiers.[1] The passage is not quite free from ambiguity, but probably all these men had first turned Muslim. 'Umar II assumed that *dhimmis* would be present in most armies.[2] In 365, Abu l 'Alā 'Ubaidulla b. Fadl, a Christian, was commander under 'Adud ud Dawla.[3] Two thousand warrior Jews lived in Tadmur, and fought against the Christians and Arabs who were subjects of Nūr ud Dīn, but helped their Muslim neighbours.[4]

Even monks must have had arms of some sort, for monasteries were able to defend themselves when attacked.[5]

It is evident that very little attention was paid to this clause of the covenant.

WITNESSES

The testimony of a *dhimmi* to what concerned a Muslim was not accepted.[6] It is reported that 'Umar II was the first to impose this disability.[7]

Some authorities were very strict. They imagined an extreme case—that of a Muslim who fell dangerously ill on a journey, and wished to make his will when there were no Muslims at hand to act as witnesses. According to one book, Abū Hanīfa, Mālik, and Shāfe'i refused to accept a *dhimmi* as witness even in such circumstances.[8] According to another, the witness of a *dhimmi* was then accepted, though Ahmad b. Hanbal added that he must swear that he has not been unfaithful, has not concealed,

---

[1] S., 164.   [2] Ibn Sa'd, 5, 262.   [3] Ecl., 2, 392.   [4] Benj., 45.
[5] B.H., 516.   [6] Mud., 4, 81.   [7] Lang., 253.   [8] Rahmat, 2,188.

changed or altered anything, and that it is the man's
will.[1] The systems of the lawyers were stricter than
common usage, for the *Lisān ul 'Arab*, in the article
on the word witness, says that the testimony of a
dhimmi to the concerns of a Muslim is accepted if
he is on a journey or in case of necessity.[2] Opinions
were divided whether the witness of one *dhimmi*
against another could be accepted. Abū Hanīfa
accepted it, Mālik and Shāfe'i did not; both views are
attributed to Ahmad.[3] Here again system was stricter
than usage; for if a *dhimmi* had wine to be taxed,
its value had to be assessed by two other *dhimmis*.[4]

Mālik gives the forms to be observed by a
dhimmi in taking an oath. It had to be taken in a
place of worship, whether synagogue, church or fire
temple. A Christian had to swear by God, not by
' God who revealed the Gospel to Jesus '. Similarly
a Jew swore by God, and not by ' God who revealed
the Law '. A certain Ka'b b. Sawār swore by God,
and put the Gospel on his head, in the sanctuary.[5]

MARRIAGE

The books of canon law have a lot to say about
the relations between Muslims and *dhimmis*. While
it is certain that the rulings of the lawyers were not
always respected, there can be no doubt that the
pressure of legal opinion did help to mould popular
feeling, and so influenced the position of the *dhimmi*.

A Muslim woman could marry none but a Muslim. This law seems never to have been broken. A

---

[1] Mizan, 2, 177.   [2] L.A., 4, 225.
[3] Rahmat, 2, 188 ; Mud., 4, 81 ; Mizan, 2, 176.
[4] Kh., 79.   [5] Mud., 4, 104.

Muslim man might not marry a pervert from religion from whose tongue had gone forth words of unbelief, a Magian, an idolater, a Zindik, or one who was converted to a religion of the book after the coming of the Prophet and was not by birth a Jew.[1]

If the wife of a *dhimmi* turned Muslim and was pregnant at the time, she was given alimony till the child was born and was paid while suckling it. If one of the parents turned Muslim, minor children were counted Muslims. Shāfe'i disapproved of the suggestion that children born outside Islam remain outside till they adopt it of their own accord. If the wife of a *dhimmi* turned Muslim after the consummation of marriage, she took the whole of the bride price; if before the consummation, the husband took half. A Christian woman married to a Muslim has to observe some of the Muslim laws on ablution; otherwise she robs her husband of his rights.[2]

If a Muslim sends away his Christian wife with a triple divorce, and she marries a Christian, who divorces her, the Muslim can marry her again when her time is up.[3] If the concubine of a Christian turns Muslim, there can be no intercourse between them, and at his death she becomes free.[4] If the wife of a Christian turns Muslim while her husband is absent on a long journey, she may either wait for his return — in case he also should have turned Muslim—or she may marry again.[5]

The lawyers held that none but a Muslim could be perfectly moral. Hence unchastity was a lesser

---

[1] Ihya, 2, 25. [2] Umm, 4, 183. [3] Umm, 4, 186.
[4] Umm, 4, 189. [5] Mud., 4, 236.

sin in a *dhimmi* than in a Muslim. So, if a Muslim committed fornication or adultery with a *dhimmi* woman he was beaten, but the woman was handed over to the people of her own religion to do what they liked with her. Any other procedure would have been interference with their privileges.[1] If a Christian man committed either of these offences they were not thought so heinous, because the offender did not receive the full legal punishment in stripes.[2] What actually happened was not in accord with the rules. The Prophet is reported to have had two Jews stoned for adultery, presumbly with Jewesses.[3] Here Jewish law was simply carried out. In 617 Abū 'Ali, the son of Ibn abi 1 Bakā, a Christian, was seized by the police with a Muslim woman, named Sitt Sharaf, in his company. He confessed that many Muslim women had come to him for his wealth's sake, among them Ishtiyāk, the wife of Ibn ul Bukhāri, the keeper of the store house. The women were put in prison, and Abū 'Ali was fined six thousand dinars.[4] In 820, in Egypt, a Christian committed adultery with a Muslim woman, and both confessed to their sin. They were stoned outside the gate Sha'ria; the woman was then buried and the man burnt.[5]

If a Christian makes a vow not to have anything to do with his wife for four months, and at the end of that time they appeal to a Muslim judge, judgment is given according to Muslim law, restitution of conjugal rights or divorce. The law recommends him to pay compensation, but cannot enforce this.

[1] Mud., 4, 400.   [2] Mud., 4, 398.   [3] Umm, 4, 186.
          [4] B.H. Mu., 419.   [5] Husn, 2, 184.

If a Christian slanders his wife and they appeal to a Muslim judge, he decides as for Muslims. If the man refuses to accept the verdict, he is beaten, but not with the full number of stripes; for the full number is not fixed as the punishment for slandering a Christian woman.[1] If the concubine of a *dhimmi* commits a crime, he can redeem her at her full value, if the damages are equal to or greater than that. If they are less, he can pay them or he can give her to the party wronged.[2]

Al Ghazāli says that a Muslim woman ought not to expose her person to a *dhimmi* woman. He assumes that this might happen in a bath used by both Muslims and *dhimmis*, men and women.[3]

TRADE

It is not necessary to repeat here what has been said in other chapters of the existence and wealth of *dhimmi* merchants. Benjamin of Tudela is careful to name the occupations of the Jews he met; they were dyers, weavers of silk, makers of Tyrian glass, and shipowners.

The lawyers did not approve of association with such people in trade. Mālik did not think it right for a Muslim to hire a garden from a Christian on a profit-sharing basis, though he might let one to a Christian on these terms ; or a vineyard, so long as no wine was made from the grapes.[4] Again he would have allowed partnership between a Muslim and a *dhimmi* only on the impossible condition that the Muslim should be present at all transactions carried through by his partner.[5] He ruled also

---

[1] Umm, 4, 184.   [2] Mud., 4, 463.   [3] Ihya, 2, 235.
[4] Mud., 4, 11, 57.   [5] Mud., 4, 38.

that a Muslim might not employ a Christian slave
in trade.[1] That these lawyers' laws were only
counsels of perfection is proved by incidents like the
following : About the year 567, the Franks captured
two Egyptian ships and seized the cargoes, but,
after energetic action by Nūr ud Dīn, restored the
goods to their owners. A merchant had some
goods on both ships in charge of two agents. When
the goods were given back each man got only a
small part of his property. Each took what belonged to him and the cloth marked by his name ; but
some took what did not belong to them. One of
the two agents, a trustworthy man and a Christian,
took only what bore his name and mark, thus losing
much of his merchandise ; indeed, he saved more of
the merchant's wares than his own. When he came
back he restored his goods to the merchant, who
refused to take them and told him to keep them all,
as he was better able to bear the loss than the agent.
He also rejected a proposal to share equally. Some
time later the agent came with some cloth belonging
to the merchant. A man from Tabriz, a passenger
on the same ship, had got back his wares, and found
among them some cloth with the agent's name on it.
He had enquired after him, searched him out, and
given his cloth back to him. ' Such men are few,'
adds the historian.[2]

Nāsir i Khusrau says that in his day there was a
Christian in Egypt who, when a famine was expected,
told the vizier that he had enough corn to feed the
whole of Cairo for six years.[3]

---

[1] Mud., 4, 128.   [2] Raudatain, 1, 203.   [3] Sefernameh, 53.

Some of the lawyers' views are quite favourable to *dhimmis*. Thus if a Muslim and a Christian are part owners of a house, and the Muslim wants to sell his share, the Christian has the right of pre-emption.[1]

If a slave to whom his master has promised freedom at his death is hurt or killed, the master takes the damages.[2]

The thought that Muslims could be the slaves of *dhimmis* was not pleasant, but the lawyers did not dare to deny the *dhimmi's* right to buy any slaves he chose. The purchase was legal, but Shāfe'i would compel a Christian to sell his Muslim slave to a Muslim. In the same way, if a slave turned Muslim, his Christian owner, or part owner, should be forced to sell his slave or his share of him.[3] If the slave of a Christian turns Muslim while his master is absent on a long journey, he is to be sold.[4]

A *dhimmi* may not bring waste land under cultivation.[5]

A Muslim may not accept from a *dhimmi* wine or a pig as a pledge.[6]

He may not bequeath anything to a *dhimmi*, but he may accept as a bequest from one anything, except wine or a pig or anything that makes a Muslim liable to poll-tax.[7] It is reported that 'Abd ul Malik ordered all pigs in the towns of Syria and North Mesopotamia to be slaughtered.[8]

If a *dhimmi* promises to give something to a Muslim and then tries to back out of his promise,

---

[1] Mud., 4, 236.   [2] Mud., 4, 438.   [3] Umm, 4, 188.
[4] Mud., 4, 236.   [5] Umm, 4, 133.   [6] Mud., 4, 164.
[7] Mud., 4, 287.   [8] S.A., 1, 296 ; C.M., 232.

the Muslim can take him to law. If this happens
between two *dhimmis* there is no appeal to law.[1]

It was not thought right for a Muslim to borrow
money from a Christian.[2] This is only an example
of the general rule that a *dhimmi* must not have
power over a Muslim.

BANKING

Two Jews, Yūsuf b. Finhas (Phinehas) and
Hārūn b. 'Imrān, formed a firm of bankers in
Mesopotamia. At one time they farmed the taxes
of Ahwāz.[3] The vizier, Ibn ul Furāt, had 700,000
dinars deposited with them.[4] He also employed
them when he wished to embezzle government
money.[5] There was a guild of Jewish bankers in
Egypt.[6] The Jewish quarter of Isfahan was a great
centre of trade.[7]

WINE

History has many stories of the drinking of
wine by Muslims. It is argued that a sharp distinction was drawn between palm wine and grape
wine, the one forbidden and the other allowed; that
khamr, the foreign product, foreign as its name, was
taboo, and *nabīdh*, the indigenous article, was
allowed; and that men like the caliph Hārūn drank
only palm wine. According to the *Lisān ul'Arab*, no
argument can be based on the word used. *Nabīdh*
might mean the non-intoxicating fresh palm juice,
but it was also used for any intoxicating liquor. It
is probable that many Muslims drank grape wine,

[1] Mud., 4, 330.   [2] Mud., 4, 11, 57.   [3] Viziers, 178.
[4] 'Arib., 74.   [5] Viziers, 78 f.   [6] Mez., 449.   [7] Muk., 388.

13

and it is certain that many were, according to later standards, very lax in their attitude towards it.

The covenant says that no *dhimmi* shall sell wine to a Muslim or show it in public. The opinion of Shāfe'i is that, if a *dhimmi* sells wine to a Muslim, the government has to annul the sale, confiscate the price if it has been already paid, pour out the wine, and punish the seller.[1] All this is unknown in the first century.

Thus Bishr b. Marwān, among other gifts, sent wine to al Akhtal.[2] When Sha'bi visited Kūfa he was asked to dine and drink wine with the Christian poet,[3] who once came into the presence of 'Abd ul Malik, his beard dripping with wine.[4] Speech was free to an extent not possible later. Al Akhtal said to Mutawakkil ul Laithi, ' If I poured wine into you, you would be the best of all poets.'[5] The exploits of some topers have been recorded and the literary world does not seem to have been shocked at them. Thus al Ukaishir passed by a woman in Hīra who sold wine, and said to her, ' Give me good measure and I will give you good praise.'[6] The same man was compelled to join an army that went to fight the people of Syria. He rode on a donkey as he had no horse, and, lagging behind, came to a village where was a tavern kept by a Nabataean. He hid there, sold his donkey, and spent the price on drink and the wife of the innkeeper.[7]

Among the papyri is an order, dated 82, for wine for the household of the governor.[8] This may have been for the use of the Christian members of the

---

[1] Umm, 4, 131.   [2] Agh., 10, 2.   [3] Agh., 8, 81.   [4] Agh., 7, 169.
[5] Agh., 11, 37.   [6] Agh., 10, 86.   [7] Agh., 10, 90.   [8] B.M., 4, 1375.

household. Boiled wine occurs regularly in the tax lists and requisition forms; it is probably the vinegar of the Arabic texts.

'Umar II forbade the use of wine, and gave orders to break the wine jars and shut the taverns.[1] The prohibition had very little effect. Even caliphs were not too pious to provide wine for those who wanted it. Mansūr thought that Jurjis b. Bukhtishu' was not looking well, so had some special wine fetched for him. Once when Yuhannā b. Māsaweih was drinking with al Wāthik, he was given bad wine because he had failed to tip the cup-bearer. He told the caliph that it was his business to know the taste of things, but he had never tasted anything like that wine. He contrived to get three hundred thousand dirhams out of the caliph as compensation.[2]

The papyri show that Muslims took part in the wine trade, both directly and indirectly. In one a certain Yazīd reports the purchase and carriage to Fustāt of a quantity of wine, and the payment of duty on it.[3] One Ahmad b. 'Umar b. Sarī' received half a dinar from Stephanus, being six months' rent of a tavern.[4] In the third century the 'taxes of enjoyment', in other words, taxes on wine, in Nisibis produced five thousand dinars yearly.[5] In the next century there were heavy taxes on taverns in Shiraz.[6] In Karaj, the trade in wine produced four hundred thousand dirhams for the revenue.[7]

The accounts of the festivals in Egypt show how important the wine trade was. Al Hākim forbade the sale of intoxicants.[8] Baibars made several

[1] K., 68.   [2] Tabak., 1, 175.   [3] Rainer, 161.   [4] Rainer, 630.
[5] I.H., 142.   [6] Muk., 429.   [7] Yak.B., 273.   [8] M., 2, 287.

attempts to stop the trade. In 663 he forbade the sale and brewing of beer in Egypt.[1] In 666 he poured away the wine in Cairo. And again i n 669 he poured away the wine and stopped the monopoly which had brought into the treasury a thousand dinars yearly.[2]

[1] Q., 2, 5.   [2] M., 1, 106.

CHAPTER XIII

TAXATION

IN legal terminology, *kharāj* means land tax and *jizya* poll-tax. It has been proved conclusively, and here it is only needful to mention the fact, that this usage is not primitive, and that both words, *kharāj* in the east and *jizya* in Egypt, meant tribute. The commonly accepted tradition is that 'Umar I imposed two taxes, land and poll, which were uniform throughout the empire.

Information about taxation is found in the papyri, historical works, law books, and those written for the instruction of secretaries.

THE PAPYRI

Among the papyri discovered in Egypt are many dealing with taxation, for the most part between the years 80 and 100. There are lists of payments by individuals, tax rolls, notifications of taxes due, requisitions, and details of sums paid by persons and institutions. Many of these papers are fragmentary, fail us when we most want their aid, and take for granted what we most want to know. Still some things are clear. There were several taxes. The land paid both money and corn, though it is not clear whether these were two separate taxes or parts of one; the *tetartia* paid in money; requisitions which seem to have been paid usually in money; special requisitions of milk and honey; and the poll-tax. No Muslim is recorded as paying taxes.

This might be chance but, considering the testimony of Muslim historians, it is certain that they did not pay.

POLL-TAX

There is no record of a woman paying poll-tax, which agrees with the statements of the historians and lawyers. Not all men paid it. Some priests paid, but others did not (1420; 38 f., 47, 49, 77).[1] Sons and children (presumably grown up) paid while other children (presumably minors) did not (1420; 39, 45, 87). There is no evidence that monks paid. The rate of assessment varied, it was 3 dinars (1427, 5; 1428, 6), $2\frac{1}{2}$ (1428, 5), and 4 (1428, 11). Easement was given by assessing a man as a fraction of a person, so 9 men are counted as $8\frac{1}{3}$ (1427, 5). In A.H. 195 a baker paid $\frac{1}{2}$ dinar (670).

A few totals will show the amounts actually paid.

95 men pay 230 dinars.	7 men pay $20\frac{1}{2}$ dinars.
5 ,, ,, $7\frac{1}{6}$,,	5 ,, ,, 13 ,,
7 ,, ,, 17 ,,	12 ,, ,, $25\frac{1}{6}$,,
15 ,, ,, $38\frac{1}{2}$,,	44 ,, ,, $108\frac{2}{3}$,,

(1420; 3, 146 f.)

LAND TAX

The land paid both cash and corn; for convenience we may call the latter payment the corn tax. Landholders, including women, paid this tax, and some who had no land even paid the corn tax. Tradesmen paid a special tax, apparently in place of the land tax. Corn land and vineyards were registered separately, and probably at different rates (1339). The palms and acacias were counted (577).

---

[1] In the references to papyri, numbers below 1,000 refer to Rainer, those above to B.M.

The rate of the land tax varied; often it was 1 dinar on 4 *aroura*, though it might be as low as ⅔ or as high as 1⅛. In one case 3·4 *aroura* of irrigated land, and 5·1 of unirrigated, each paid 1 dinar (1428).

Some leases of crown lands of a later date may serve for comparison. (The last three were certainly granted to Muslims.)

Forty *feddān*, at a rent of 30 dinars, for 10 *feddān* were without water and not taxable. A.H. 176 (621).

Fifty *feddān*, at a rent of 50 dinars, and payment in kind. A.H. 177 or 178 (625).

One dinar, 10 *ardebb* of wheat, and 3⅓ *ardebb* of barley for the *feddān*. No date. (626.)

One dinar and 15 *ardebb* of wheat the *feddān* for wheat land, and 1 dinar, ½ *ardebb* of wheat, and ⅙ *ardebb* of barley for land under barley. A.H. 180 (638).

At the end of the first century most of the holdings seem to have been small; the biggest sum paid by an individual was 7 dinars. The following prices and wages will be useful for estimating the real value of money. In A.H. 80, twenty *ardebb* of wheat cost 1 dinar, and in A.H. 88, twelve cost 1 dinar, while later, 10 *ardebb* of wheat, or 20 of barley, cost 1 dinar (587, 1433, 1434). In A.H. 92, one sheep cost ½ dinar (1375).

A shipbuilder for wages and expenses got 2 dinars a month.
A caulker   ,,   ,,   ,,   ,,   ,, 1½   ,,   ,, (1410)
A carpenter   ,,   ,   ,,   ,,   ,, ⅔   ,,   ,, (1336)
A sawyer got 11 dinars yearly, a labourer 16, and a carpenter 23 (1341, 1366).

In A.H. 88 the corn tax was roughly 1 *ardebb* for every dinar of the land tax (1420), but in 96 (?) it was 2 *ardebb* to the dinar (1424).

In 98 and the five following years the land tax of Aphrodite (Ashkuh) remained constant at 6951 dinars, 15 carats, i.e. $\frac{15}{24}$. It was not always so. In 80, Psurou (Basīrū) paid 70 dinars 21 c., and in 91 it paid 104$\frac{1}{3}$ (1412 and Der Islam 2, 267).

The following list shows how payments varied:

	A.H. 80–85		A.H. 91
Pakaunis	371	din.	498 din.
Empheuteuon	390	,,	131$\frac{1}{3}$,,
Bounon	40	,,	47$\frac{1}{6}$,,
Keranios	50	,,	25$\frac{1}{3}$,,
Poimen	102	,,	30$\frac{1}{3}$,,
Monastery of Mary ..	114	,,	98 ,,
Monastery of Pharos ..	111	,,	5$\frac{5}{8}$,,
Monastery of Mary ..	48	,,	47$\frac{1}{2}$,,
3 Pediades	436$\frac{1}{3}$	,,	400$\frac{5}{8}$,,
2 Pediades	233	,,	253$\frac{1}{6}$,,
5 Pediades	421	,,	461$\frac{1}{2}$,,
Monastery of Barbaros ..	110	,,	10 ,,

(1412–1419. P.S.R. Appendix)

	A.H. 88	A.H. 97
Desert Monastery of Mary	30$\frac{1}{4}$ din.	114 din.
Abba Ermaotos ..	28$\frac{1}{8}$,,	189$\frac{1}{3}$,,

It is clear from these figures that some of the monasteries were rich; the desert monastery of Mary had eight estates in A.H. 98, and that of Barbaros had ten (1419).

The central government notified a district how much it had to pay, and local officials distributed the sum among the taxpayers. A typical notice is, ' From Kurra b. Shuraik to the people of Psurou. Your share of the tribute for the year 88 is 104$\frac{1}{3}$ dinars, and of the corn tax 11$\frac{1}{3}$ *ardebb* wheat. Written by Rashīd, Safar 91.' It seems that the lunar year 91 was the solar year 88.[1]

[1] Caetani, Vol. IV, pl. v.

TETARTIA

This was about one per cent of the land tax.

It is noteworthy that 609 has a list of three money taxes, and a Syriac historian speaks of taxes, tribute and poll-tax.[1]

REQUISITIONS

fall into two classes: those 'included in the schedule' and 'those not included'. The 'included' requisitions bear no fixed proportion to the land tax; but vary from one-half in the case of Sakoore to one-ninety-second in the case of Pakaunis. The 'not included' vary even more (1413). The requisitions for milk and honey were not levied on the smaller sub-divisions. Indeed, the smaller places seem to have been burdened only with the bigger, more general, requisitions. The following table shows the requisitions on three monasteries:

	Holy Mary	Barbaros	Abba Ermaotos
Allowance for the Commander of the Faithful	—	—	—
Goods for the boats	$\frac{2}{3}$	—	$\frac{2}{3}$
Cloth for a hair tent	$\frac{5}{12}$	$\frac{1}{12}$	? $\frac{5}{12}$
Fine	$33\frac{1}{16}$	—	$28\frac{1}{3}$
Half sailor for the fleet, expenses, and 2 measures of boiled wine for the Muhajirun	$\frac{1}{2}$	$\frac{1}{2}$	$\frac{1}{2}$
Two measures of boiled wine for the Muhajirun of the fleet	$\frac{3}{4}$	$\frac{1}{2}$	—
Carriage of goods for the boats at Klysma	$\frac{1}{6}$	$\frac{1}{6}$	$\frac{1}{3}$
Pile for embankment	$\frac{1}{6}$	—	—
Expenses of governor	$\frac{5}{6}$	$\frac{1}{2}$	$\frac{5}{6}$

[1] C.M., 335.

	Holy Mary	Barbaros	Abba Ermaotos
Care of embankment	$\frac{1}{4}$	?	—
Goods for Klysma	—	$\frac{1}{8}$	$\frac{1}{4}$
Sailor for Anatolian fleet, and expenses	—	—	$\frac{1}{4}$
Forty workmen for the mosque at Damascus	—	—	$\frac{1}{2}$
Care of embankment, baskets ..	50	20	?
Money total. dinars	$36\frac{1}{12}$	$2\frac{1}{4}$	$31\frac{2}{3}$

(A.H. 88, 1433)

Contributions are often mentioned. It is not certain if these were the same as the requisitions or not. From the Rainer collection come the following: '20 *ardebb* of barley (551), 3,164 *ardebb* of wheat (A.H. 21, 553), 3 meals for men (555), 342 *ardebb* of wheat and 171 measures of oil for 342 soldiers and 12 armourers' (?) (557). This last reminds one curiously of 'Umar's method of finding out how much was wanted by the soldiers as rations. Then 65 sheep (558) and 99 horses (564) are called for. In A.H. 91 is a demand for 70 *camisia* at $\frac{1}{4}$ dinar each, for 'the subsidy of the Commander of the Faithful' (1362). Divers articles of food are wanted by the governor 'for the maintenance of us, and the officials who are with us, both Arabs and Christians, and of various persons . . . '(1375). Many sailors were wanted for the fleets, and the taxpayers had to provide their wages; hence the frequent occurrence in the accounts of half a sailor or some other fraction, the district having to provide that part of his wages. Labourers had to be supplied for work in Jerusalem and Damascus, and their wages paid.

At this time many of the Egyptian peasants fled from their holdings. It is safe to assume that one reason for their doing so was the burden of taxation.

It is obvious that there are serious discrepancies between the account given by the lawyers and that of the papyri. The latter prove the existence of taxes which are not even hinted at by the legal system.

THE HISTORIANS

The terms given to the various places conquered were not on a model imposed from Medina, but depended on local conditions and the temper of the victor. For the sake of completeness, terms imposed by the Prophet, whether historical or legendary, are included in the following list of treaties.

The Prophet wrote to Bahrain, ' Whoso prays facing in the same direction as we do, and eats what we kill, is a Muslim with the same privileges and duties as we have. Whoso does not do this must pay one dinar in Ma'āfiri cloaks.' [1]

Some of the people of Bahrain made peace, promising to pay half their dates and corn. [2]

Every adult male in Bahrain paid one dinar, [3] in Yemen one dinar or its value in cloth. In Yemen both men and women paid a dinar. [4]

A male *dhimmi* in Yemen paid one dinar. A governor tried to take one-fifth of the crops, but was not allowed to. A Christian living in Mecca paid one dinar a year. [5]

The terms with Nejrān were: (1) the payment of 2,000 cloaks of the average value of 40 dirhams weight of silver; any deficiency could be made good in horses, camels, arms, or provisions; (2) the entertaining of the Prophet's messengers for a

---

[1] Kh., 75. [2] B., 80. [3] B., 81. [4] B., 71. [5] Umm, 4, 101.

month; (3) the supply of 30 horses, 30 camels, and
30 coats of mail in the event of war in Yemen; these
were to be made good by the Prophet if destroyed.
The tribute of cloaks was diminished by 'Uthmān,
and by subsequent caliphs, as the numbers of the
Nejrānis decreased.[1]

On his return to Medina from Tebūk, the Prophet
imposed a tax on the *dhimmi* in Medina, Mecca,
Khaibar, Yemen, and Nejrān, 1 dinar or there-
abouts on the men, and nothing on the women and
children.[2]

He levied 1 dinar a head on Tebūk and Aila.[3]

In the reign of Abū Bakr almost the first place
outside Arabia to be conquered was Bosra; there
every adult male had to pay 1 dinar and 1 *jarīb* of
wheat.[4] The same terms were given to Antioch
later.[5]

Banikia paid 1,000 dinars and a *tailasān*.[6]

In the reign of 'Umar conquests became rapid.
Many traditions refer to Syria, but it is impossible
to know whether they mean Damascus or Syria as
a whole.

At first every one paid 1 dinar and 1 *jarīb*, but
later 'Umar changed this.

Khālid imposed on Damascus 1 dinar, 1 *jarīb*, and
oil and vinegar.[7] Abū 'Ubaida imposed a fixed
tribute, not to be increased if they multiplied, not
to be diminished if they became fewer.[8] Two dinars
a head and food. Some were taxed according to their
ability to pay; if their wealth increased so did the
tax, if it diminished the additional tax was dropped.[9]

---

[1] B., 64.   [2] Suli, 214.   [3] B., 59.   [4] B., 113.   [5] B., 147.
[6] B., 244.   [7] B., 124.   [8] I.A., 1, 178.   [9] I.A., 1, 150.

On adult males 4 dinars, 2 *mudd* wheat, 3 *kist*
oil, and the duty of entertaining Muslim travellers
for three days.[1] Another version makes the wheat
and oil a monthly payment, adds to these ghee and
honey, and omits the entertainment.[2]

In Rakka every man paid 1 dinar, several *kaɉiz*
of wheat, vinegar, oil, and honey.[3]

In Edessa every man paid 1 dinar and 2 *mudd* of
wheat.[4]

In al Jazīra—North Mesopotamia—tribute was at
first paid in kind, food, oil, and vinegar. Then
'Umar reduced this, and introduced the graduated
poll-tax, with 2 *mudd* of wheat and 2 *kist* each of oil
and vinegar.[5] Another version is 1 dinar, 2 *mudd*
of wheat, and 2 *kist* each of oil and vinegar, and that
'Abd ul Malik raised it to 4 dinars without grading.[6]

Bārūsmā and az Zawābi agreed to pay 4 dirhams
a head. Bārūsmā broke faith and was sacked.[7] This
resembles the story that Constantine, the patrician
of Syria, told 'Umar that the terms imposed by Abū
'Ubaida were 4 dirhams and a cloak a head. He
afterwards confessed that this was his own invention.[8]
It also resembles the treaty made by 'Ishoyahbh,
whereby the rich paid 12 dirhams, and the poor,
except priests, paid 4.[9] It is curious that the figure
4 occurs later. Tamīm abū Harrāb rebelled against
Mu'tasim in Palestine, and was followed by 30,000
of the hungry and naked. According to Michael the
Syrian, who calls him Thamam, he declared that
Christians should pay only a tax of 4 dirhams.[10]

[1] B., 152. [2] B., 125. [3] B., 173. [4] B., 174. [5] B., 178.
[6] Kh., 23. [7] B., 251. [8] Ghazi, 389. [9] B.H., Eccl., 3, 115 f.
[10] Lang., 275 ; cf. B.H., 152.

There is a story, that is almost unbelievable, but yet is too curious to have been invented. The tribe of Bajīla formed a quarter of the army which fought at Kādisia, so 'Umar promised them a quarter of the Sawād—South Mesopotamia. Finally he persuaded their chief, Jarīr b. 'Abdulla, to surrender his claims—according to one story, after he had enjoyed them for three years—for 80 or, in another version, 400 dinars. A woman refused to give up her share till 'Umar gave her a pure bred camel, with a red saddle cloth, and filled her hands with gold. Another version is that, after the battle of Jalūlā, Jarīr gave up his rights at the caliph's request. Yet another says that every man of the tribe received a pension of 2,000.[1]

Other places paid lump sums. Hīra paid 80,000 or 100,000 dirhams yearly.[2] Yahya says, ' Terms were made with the men of Hīra to pay a sum which they distributed among themselves; there was no fixed amount on the individual.' [3]

Anbār paid 400,000 dirhams and 1,000 cloaks.[4]

Edessa and Harrān paid fixed sums.[5] Hims paid 170,000 dinars according to one story, but Tabari says that some of the inhabitants paid 1 dinar and food.[6]

The Samaritans at first paid poll-tax. Yazīd b. Mu'āwia made them pay land tax, and put a poll-tax of 2 dinars on those in the Jordan province and 5 on those in Palestine. Some of them appealed to Mutawakkil, and he cut it down from 5 to 3.[7]

When Tiflis was captured, in the reign of

---

[1] B., 267 f.; Umm, 4, 192.   [2] B., 243.   [3] Yahya, 36.   [4] B., 246.
[5] Kh., 23.   [6] B., 130; T.I., 2391; Azdi, 128.   [7] B., 158.

'Uthmān, each family agreed to pay 1 dinar, both sides promising to play fair in counting families.[1]

In the treaty made by Surāka, in 22, with the people of Armenia and the Gates, it was arranged that they should join the Muslim armies, and military service take the place of tribute. Those who did not join the army had to pay the same tribute as the people of Adherbaijān.[2]

In al Jazīra the villagers were treated exactly as the townspeople, except that they had to supply rations to the Muslims.[3]

Egypt. The traditions are many. Two dinars on every male.[4] Two dinars a head and food for the Muslims.[5] Two dinars and food. The food was later compounded for at the rate of 2 dinars, making a tax of 4.[6] Two dinars on every adult male and on 1 *jarīb*, 1 dinar, and 3 *ardebb* of food.[7] Two dinars on every male except the poor, and on every landowner 3 *ardebb* of wheat, and 2 *kist* each of oil, honey, and vinegar. All had to provide clothing for the army, shoes, trousers, turbans, coats, and cloaks.[8] As Sūli gives the same tribute without the clothing.[9]

The graded money tax, 12 *ardebb* of wheat yearly and three days' entertainment of Muslims.[10]

It is said that 'Amr imposed a tax of 26⅔ dirhams on all, and on the rich 2 dinars and 3 *ardebb* of wheat.[11] This is intelligible if the second tax was in addition to the first, when the rich would have paid about twice as much as the poor.

[1] B., 201.   [2] T.I., 2665.   [3] Kh., 23.   [4] M., 1, 76.   [5] M., 1, 294.
[6] B., 216.   [7] B. 215.   [8] B., 214.   [9] Suli, 217.
[10] B., 125 ; M., 1, 76.   [11] A.S., 75.

It is definitely stated that the Copts paid to the Muslims the same tribute they had paid to the Byzantines.[1]

The general impression gained from these traditions is that the larger part of the tribute was derived from a poll-tax. The papyri show that the poll-tax was a smaller item than the land tax.

It was held that if a town had capitulated, the terms of the capitulation were binding on the Muslims, whereas they were free to do as they liked with one that had been captured by force of arms. There was much discussion whether Egypt had capitulated or not. The discussion was purely academic, though traditions were quoted on both sides. Mu'āwia tried to add to the tribute of Egypt, but the attempt was foiled by the refusal of Wardān, a freedman of 'Amr's.[2] On the other side this tale is told. The headman of Ikhna came ·to 'Amr and said, ' Tell us what tribute each one has to pay and we will pay it.' 'Amr pointed to a corner of the church, and said, ' If you gave me that, filled with money from the floor to the roof, I would not tell you what you have to pay. You are our treasury. If we need much, you will pay much, if our burdens are small, so will yours be.'[3] Not all accounts of 'Amr are flattering. A Christian says that he was of savage extraction, treated the Egyptians without pity, and did not keep the treaties he had made.[4] He is said to have left 70 skins of dinars, each weighing 2 Egyptian *ardebb*. His sons refused to take this money until those to whom any of it might belong

---

[1] M., 1, 76.　　[2] B., 217.　　[3] M., 1, 77, 168.　　[4] J.N., 377.

had received their due share. Mu'āwia took it.[1] In
this same period 'Umar fined several of his governors for enriching themselves at the expense of the
provincials ; they were Sa'd b. abī Wakkās of Kūfa,
'Amr of Egypt, Abū Huraira of Bahrain, Nu'mān b.
'Adi of Maisān, Nāfi' b. 'Amr of Mecca, and Ya'la b.
Munya of Yemen.[2]

At a later date a caliph is made to testify to the
sufferings of the *dhimmis*. A Muslim said to 'Umar
II, ' Commander of the Faithful, why are prices high
in your reign when they were low in those preceding ? ' He replied, ' Those before me burdened the
dhimmis above their strength, so that they were
obliged to sell their goods at a loss. I lay on them
a burden they can bear, so that they can sell when
they please.' The man said, ' I wish you would fix
prices for us.' The caliph answered, ' This is not
our business ; God fixes prices.'[3] But the order
attributed to him, ' Leave to those on the Euphrates,
who pay tribute enough to let them have gold seals,
to wear the *tailasān*, and to ride on hackneys. Take
what is left over ',[4] gives a less favourable view of
his rule.

There can be no doubt that the tribute of Egypt—
and probably of other provinces—was increased.
'Abdulla b. abī Sarh extracted a bigger revenue
than did 'Amr, though the figures twelve and fourteen millions are exaggerated, and 'Amr's defence
before the caliph is famous. Other increases are
mentioned. While 'Abd ul 'Azīz was governor, a
census of the monks was taken and they were made

---

[1] M., 1, 301. [2] Yak., 2, 181 ; B., 82, 384. [3] Kh., 76.
[4] Uyun, 1, 53.

to pay 1 dinar each.[1] Severus says, ' This was the first *jizya*.' It is not clear whether he means the first poll-tax or the first tribute paid by monks.

As Sūli has an account that deserves to be quoted in full. ' These terms were given them; their wives, children, estates, and houses were not to be sold, their treasures not confiscated, and no addition made to their tribute. This continued till 'Abdulla b. Sa'd b. abī Sarh became governor; he raised two million of revenue till the reign of 'Abd ul Malik, who made his brother 'Abd ul 'Azīz governor of Egypt. He made a survey of the estates —which were many—and gave fiefs to some soldiers. This added to the burden on the payers of poll-tax, who were asked to pay a million dinars. They went to 'Abd ul Malik and complained. When they came back 'Abd ul 'Azīz added to their tribute.'[2]

The tribute was increased by two-thirds; no date is given.[3]

Kurra b. Shuraik added 100,000 dinars to the tribute.[4]

Usāma made each monk pay 1 dinar.

'Umar II freed the estates of the church and the bishops from *kharāj*, but Yazīd restored these taxes.[5]

In the reign of Hishām the tribute was doubled.[6]

Ibn ul Habhāb increased the tribute by one-eighth or one-twenty-fourth.[7]

Abu l Kāsim doubled the tribute.[8]

In 167 Mūsā b. Mus'ab doubled what was taken from each *feddān*, and laid taxes on those who had stalls in the markets and on animals.[9] This was

---

[1] M., 2, 492; S., 134.   [2] Suli, 217.   [3] S., 136.   [4] S., 140.   [5] S., 143.
[6] S., 145.   [7] S., 150; K. 73; M., 2, 492.   [8] S., 155, 163.   [9] K., 125.

evidently part of the policy of the caliph Hārūn, who added to the tribute of the Christians so that many emigrated and fled from their estates, leaving them in the hands of the Arabs.[1]

Another increase was made in 213.[2]

The phrase, 'doubled the tribute', is so common that clearly it is not to be taken literally. Even if Christian evidence is suspect, there is enough Muslim testimony to prove that the tribute of Egypt was made heavier.

METHODS OF ASSESSMENT

The mode of assessment, outlined in the demand notes of the governor preserved among the papyri, is described by Makrīzi, following Ibn 'Abd ul Hakam. This account takes the original assessment for granted, and treats of increases only. The method is the same. "'Amr, when he was sure of the tribute (or, had received assurances from the officials), fixed for the Copts the tribute paid before to the Greeks. That had been allotted justly. If a village had been cultivated and populous, the tribute had been increased; if the people were few and the land neglected, it was diminished. Those who knew the villages, the officials, and the heads of the people came together and examined the state of cultivation; then, if they decided on an increase, they allotted this between the districts. They met the village headmen, and divided it according to the capacity of the villages and the extent of their fields. Then each one took its share (of the increase), and combined it with the tribute and the cultivated

[1] S.A., 2, 3.   [2] K., 185.

area. They began by subtracting two *feddāns* from the total area for their churches, carts, and boats; then they subtracted enough to meet the entertainment of Muslims and visits of the ruler. Next they estimated the number of workmen and hirelings in each village, and gave them shares according to their ability. If there were any fugitives (from other places) they were given shares equal to their ability. A share was seldom given except to young or married men. Then they took what was left of the tribute, and divided it among themselves in proportion to the size of their holdings. Then a re-arrangement was made for those who were ready to cultivate according to their capacity. If a man could not cultivate his land and pleaded inability, they gave what he could not work to those who could; and he who was ready to do more than his share supplied the deficiences of the weak. If they acted stingily towards each other, division was made according to their preparedness. The basis of the division was the twenty-four *kirats* in the dinar.

' Each *feddān* paid ½ *ardebb* of wheat and 2 *waiba*, that is 12 *mudd*, of barley. Clover (or, mimosa leaves for tanning) was not taxed. 'Umar took from tributaries the appointed sum, neither more nor less. He considered the case of those who surrendered on condition of paying tribute though no sum had been fixed; if needful, he fixed it low, but if they were rich he made it higher.'[1]

It is well to emphasize certain points in this description. The agreement with the papyri has already been noted. Land is held by the commune rather

---

[1] M., 1, 77.

than by individuals. Fugitives, who have tried to escape the burden of taxation, do not succeed in doing so entirely. Certain fields are set apart to meet the cost of public works, but this does not mean any lightening of the burden of tribute, for it presses more heavily on the remaining land. The entertainment of Muslims is a communal matter, not a private one, as is suggested by most references to this duty. In its emphasis on the fairness and the good temper of the proceedings, it reads like a rescript from the governor.

LAND TAX

Men who pay tribute are of three sorts: landowners, who pay out of the produce of the land, craftsmen, who pay out of their earnings, and merchants, who deal in money and pay out of their profits; as payers of tribute they are all in the same class.[1] This statement by 'Umar II agrees with the papyri, which show that tradesmen paid a special tax in place of the land tax.

Most detailed accounts of the land tax refer to Mesopotamia. A selection of them follows. The unit of measurement is always the *jarīb*, a square of 60 cubits side, the area sown by a *jarīb*, a measure of capacity.

One dirham and 1 *kafīz*. ' He left them the palms for their own use.'[2]

Vineyards	10 dir.[3]		Vineyards	10 dir.[4]
Palms	5 „	(10 B.)	Vegetables	6 „
Sugarcane	6 „		Sesame	5 „
Wheat	4 „		Summer greens	3 „
Barley	2 „		Cotton	5 „

[1] Umar, 99.   [2] B., 269 ; Suli, 218.   [3] B., 269 ; Suli, 218.   [4] Suli, 218.

Peas, vineyards, sesame, vegetables, 8 dir.

Palms were not taxed.

Vineyards and vegetables, 10 dir.   Wheat, 2 dir., 2 *jarīb*.[1]

Cotton   5   dir.   Barley 1 dir., 1 *jarīb*.

One palm (*farisi*) 1 ,,   Bad land $\frac{1}{2}$,,

One palm (*dikla*) $\frac{1}{2}$,,

Rough wheat $1\frac{1}{2}$ din. and 1 *sā'*.

Medium wheat   1 ,,

Fine wheat $\frac{2}{3}$,,

Barley paid about half these rates and vegetables, etc., were free. Gardens (palms, fruit trees, vineyards), 10 dirhams.[2]

These lists all agree with the statement that the tribute of Mesopotamia was fixed by 'measurement' (*masāḥa*).

The figures are very different from those given by Ibn Hawkal for Persia, where the tribute was also by 'measurement'. Taxes were heaviest in Shiraz. His figures are for the big *jarīb*, $3\frac{2}{3}$ of the small *jarīb*.

Wheat and barley (watered by streams) ..   170   dir.

Trees (watered by streams)   ..   ..   192 ,,

Vegetables (watered by streams)   .. $237\frac{2}{3}$,,

Vineyards (watered by streams)   .. 1,425 ,,

In Kuvār taxes were two-thirds of the above. There had been no tax on vines and fruit trees in the plains till 302, when 'Ali b. 'Isā b. ul Jarrāh imposed the land tax.[3]

Ibn Hawkal also says that in Egypt Jawhar, the minister of Al Mu'izz, made the rate 7 dinars on the *feddān*; before it had been $3\frac{1}{2}$.[4]

In part of Upper Egypt, the corn tax had been at the time of the Fatimids 3 *ardebb* on the *feddān*, in 572 it was $2\frac{1}{2}$, and later 2.[5]

---

[1] B., 270.   [2] B., 271.   [3] I.H., 216.   [4] I.H., 108.   [5] M., 1, 101.

Kalkashandi says that in Upper Egypt the *feddān*
of wheat paid 2 or 3 *ardebb*, and 1, 2, or 3 dirhams
with every *ardebb*. Sometimes money only was
paid. In the Delta money only was paid till 570;
the best land paid 40 dirhams and second quality 30.
Later the tax was raised to 100 dirhams and 80. In
810 a *feddān* of the best land paid 400 or even 600
dirhams. Other land paid in proportion.[1]

Some comment is necessary. The *kaj īz* was either
$\frac{1}{6}$ or $\frac{1}{10}$ of the *jarīb*. Now a crop may be anything
from thirteen to twenty-five times the amount of seed
sown. So the tax in kind, if it were one *kafīz*, would
be, at the highest estimate, one-seventy-eighth part,
or one hundred and one-thirtieth of the crop. The
addition of the dirham to be paid in money would
not bring the tax anywhere near the tithe which the
Muslim farmer paid. A tax of two *jarīb* (capacity)
sounds more reasonable. Ibn Hawkal's figures
seem to err on the other side; especially the tax on
vineyards, unless the policy of the government was
to tax them out of existence. It is impossible to
believe that palms were tax free. Possibly, in those
parts where isolated trees only were found, there
was no tax on them. It is definitely said that solitary palms, regarded as common property, were not
taxed.[2] It is more likely that the figures, one dinar
or a half on each palm, according to the quality of
the tree, are right. The Turkish government levied
a tax of seven piastres on each tree, though they are
said to have been not over-careful in counting them.

[1] Subh., 3, 453. [2] B., 271.

POLL-TAX

Most of the information about the poll-tax comes from the lawyers. Books usually say that it was graduated, four, two, or one dinar in lands with a gold currency, that is Syria and Egypt, while where silver was current the dinar was reckoned at twelve dirhams, in Mesopotamia and Persia. Another theory makes the dinar equal to ten dirhams. This system is too simple; the differences of the schools show that this amount of agreement is fictitious.

The views of the four imāms are these:

Abū Hanīfa says that the poll-tax is fixed at 12, 24, and 48 dirhams.

Ahmad b. Hanbal says that it is not fixed, but is at the discretion of the ruler. Another version of his teaching is, that the lower limit is fixed but not the upper.

Mālik says that it is fixed at 4 dinars or 40 dirhams. Probably he mentions the highest rate only, and takes the others for granted.

Shāfe'i says that it is fixed, 1 dinar on rich and poor alike.

These differences reflect different local conditions. Sha'rāni says this definitely, for he writes, ' These differences are due to the fact that the imāms take into account the conditions prevailing in the countries in which they live '.

If a man were too poor to pay the lowest rate, Shāfe'i held that he should be banished. The other three held that he should be excused payment.[1] Another writer says that he who cannot pay the graded tax should be given relief.[2]

[1] Mizan, 2, 161.   [2] Yahya, 9.

From this statement of the lawyers' views, it is clear that the commonly accepted history is a later systematization.

Opinions differed as to who paid. Abū Yūsuf says that women, boys, the poor in receipt of alms, the indigent blind, the paralyzed, and the aged did not pay. Some add to this list servants, lunatics, and men who live in cells. On the other hand, Shāfe'i held that the paralyzed, aged, blind, monks, and hired servants paid.[1] In one place the *Kitāb ul Umm* assumes that women may at times pay.[2] Hasan ul Basri said, 'Monks pay no *jizya* because they are poor and have left the world.'[3] In the treaty of 'Ishoyahbh, it is stipulated that poor priests and monks shall not pay tribute.[4] Ibn 'Abd ul Hakam knows that monks pay no taxes, for '*dhimmis* have to bear the tribute of those of them who turn monks'.[5] Abū Yūsuf says that rich monks were taxed. If a convent had estates or property in trust, the father superior paid for the monks under him. If he pleaded poverty, he was allowed to take an oath valid in his religion, and was excused payment.[6] Theodosius, a Chalcedonian Christian, who held high office in Alexandria, was an enemy of the Coptic patriarch Agatho, and made him pay thirty-six dinars *jizya* for his disciples. Presumably these were monks, so we may conclude that at that time it was not usual for monks to pay tribute.[7] It has already been said that in Egypt 'Abd ul 'Azīz made the monks pay *jizya*, while Usāma's action was to prevent men escaping tribute by becoming monks. 'Ali b. 'Isā

---

[1] Kh., 69 ; Mizan, 2, 160.   [2] Umm, 4, 98.   [3] Suli, 216.
[4] B.H. Eccl., 3, 115 f.   [5] Hakam, 156.   [6] Kh., 69.   [7] S., 113.

wished to take the *jizya* from bishops, monks, and poor Christians, but the caliph Muktadir stopped him.[1]

ENTERTAINMENT OF MUSLIMS

The rules for this varied. Where there was a gold currency they had to be entertained for three days, but in South Mesopotamia only for a day and a night. The food to be supplied was bread, porridge, condiments, oil, milk, ghee, cooked vegetables, fish, or meat, whatever was easy to provide. Three was the maximum number to be received.[2] Hims is said to have come under the one day and night rule.[3] If rain delayed these guests beyond the legal time, they had to pay.[4] When some *dhimmis* complained to 'Umar that these guests laid on them a burden greater than they could bear, asking for chicken and sheep, he said, ' Give them only what you yourselves eat and such of your food as is lawful for them.'[5] Māmūn gave orders to release the Christians from the duty of providing lodgings in their houses for soldiers.[6]

TAXES ON TRADE [7]

'Umar I instituted taxes on trade. The common tradition is that the rates were, for a Muslim $2\frac{1}{2}$ per cent, for a *dhimmi* 5, and for a foreigner 10. The tax was paid once a year only. Mālik, however, held, that it was paid on every trade journey. A Taghlibi or Nejrāni was on the same footing as another *dhimmi*, but a Magian was treated as a

[1] M., 2, 495 ; Eut., 2, 517.   [2] Umm, 4, 102, 104.   [3] Azdi, 152.
[4] Hakam, 152.   [5] I.A., 1, 179.   [6] S.A., 2, 15.
[7] Most of this section comes from Kh., 77 f.; M., 2, 121.

foreigner. Another tradition is that only foreigners paid this tax, at a rate of 10 per cent. Another says 10 per cent on *dhimmis*, and still another that a *dhimmi* did not pay in his own province, but every time he went outside it he paid 10 per cent.

'Umar I took from the Nabataeans 5 per cent of the wheat and oil, to encourage the transport of these goods to Medina, and 10 per cent on the pulse. A governor in the time of 'Umar took 10 per cent from the Nabataeans.[1] The author tries to reconcile these two statements, but evidently knows nothing about the matter. Another version of the same tradition is that 'Umar took 10 per cent from Copts in Medina, and 5 per cent on wheat and raisins.

The tax on slaves was 10 dirhams and on horses and camels 8.[2] The minimum taxable was 200 dirhams, 20 dinars or 20 *mithkāls*; but 'Umar II is said to have made 10 dinars the minimum for a *dhimmi*; this was the doctrine of Abū Hanīfa.

The goods of a slave were not taxed. A *dhimmi* wine merchant had to have his goods valued by two other *dhimmis*. If a *dhimmi* declared that his debts equalled the value of his goods, he paid nothing. At one time in Yemen taxes on winepresses, bridges, and roads were abolished, but had to be restored because of the loss to the revenue.

In the fourth century, in Persia, in addition to the religious taxes, there were tithes on shipping, fifths from mines and pastures, profit on the mint, tax establishments (octroi, toll bars?) in towns, storehouses, dues on salt pans and swamps, dues on the

[1] Umm., 4, 125.   [2] M., 1, 103.

sale of perfumes. The item storehouses included rent of ground, mills, and rosewater factories. Most of these taxes were the same, or nearly so, in all provinces.[1] Makrīzi gives a long list of dues that had to be paid in Egypt. Many brought in so little that they cannot have covered the cost of collection. Probably many of these existed from the earliest times.

Rabī'a b. Shurahbīl was controller of these taxes in Egypt under 'Amr b. l 'As, and Zuraik b. Hayyān in Ubulla under 'Umar II. Anas b. Sīrīn was appointed to collect them in Ubulla, but refused the post,[2] for 'the pious of an earlier generation disapproved of them'. Perhaps this disapproval may be connected with a change in the meaning of the word *maks*. Originally it was quite general, and meant tribute tax. Later it was limited to certain special dues which were not mentioned in the Koran or Traditions, and were consequently looked at askance by all good Muslims.

'Umar II is said to have abolished these dues.[3] This may be an anachronism; still it may be true, for it is evident that taxes were levied which had no place in the legal system.

Mansūr first started a tax on shops in 167, and in the same year the governor in Egypt—as part of the caliph's policy—put a tax on stalls in the market and on animals.[4]

The year 250 saw the introduction into Egypt of a monopoly of natron, and dues on grazing and fishing. Though they brought in 100,000 dinars

---

[1] I.H., 217.   [2] M., 2, 123 ; Husn, 1, 74.   [3] M., 1, 103.
[4] K., 125 ; M., 1, 103.

yearly, Ahmad b. Tūlūn abolished them. They were
introduced again under the Fatimids, and were called
maks. Saladin abolished them, but his son 'Uthmān
re-introduced them. We hear of some dues the
abolition of which was opposed by the Copts. In
801, Balbaghā abolished the rent (assessment) of the
Cattle Lake, but the Copts restored it. He also
found that some dues in Egypt brought in about
70,000 dirhams daily, that the government got no
profit from them, but that they profited the Copts
and their servants. He proposed to do away with
them, but did not succeed.[1] In 389 it was proposed
to tax certain kinds of cloth made in Baghdad, but
the opposition was so strong that the proposal had
to be dropped.[2] In 479 Malikshah abolished trade
dues and tolls in Irak.[3]

CONCLUSIONS

The methods of exaction were not as severe as
they might have been. Apparently, the subjects were
allowed considerable latitude in the payment of taxes,
for there are frequent complaints in the papyri of
delay in payment and other forms of slackness.
'Umar is said to have compelled the Nabataeans of
Syria to give some of their fruits and chaff to the
Muslims, but they were not forced to cart it for
them.[4] At times relief was given. A Copt said to
'Amr, ' If I lead you to a place whence ships can
go till they reach Mecca, will you release me and my
family from tribute? ' 'Amr agreed.[5] When Barka
was first conquered, no collector of tribute entered

[1] M., 1, 107 ; Subh., 3, 460.   [2] Ecl., 3, 336.   [3] Ath., y. 479.
      [4] I.A., 1, 179.   [5] Hakam, 166.

it : they sent the money when it was due.[1] Mr. Bell's judgment is perhaps more severe.[2] 'To sum up, while the evidence is not at present such as to justify very positive conclusions, it seems probable that the Arab government, during the first century of the Hejīra, was on the whole efficient and not noticeably oppressive, but that the nature of the fiscal system (which, be it remembered, was inherited from the Byzantine empire) tended to a constant increase in the burden of the taxpayers, and gave exceptional opportunity for the exactions of the subordinate officials.'

In later times the land tax was paid in instalments, and this was probably the case from the first.[3] The poll-tax seems to have been paid as a whole.

In Egypt, the pensions and rations of the Arabs enrolled in the *diwan*, and their families, repairs to the dykes, rations of the clerical staff, and the supply of corn for the Hedjaz were provided out of the tribute ; the balance was sent to the capital of the empire.[4]

It is to be noted that the Byzantine empire levied land, corn, and poll taxes, and its officials when travelling received free entertainment. It is at least a curious coincidence that its senators paid a tax, the three grades of which were in the proportion of four, two, and one.

The following conclusions are probable. The original terms made with the conquered places were almost forgotten. When remembered, the historians interpreted them in the light of later conditions, and so misunderstood them. The clearest example of

[1] Hakam, 171.　　[2] B.M., 4, xli.　　[3] M., 1, 405.　　[4] M., 1, 79.

this process is the words *kharāj* and *jizya*, which both meant tribute.

'Umar's settlement was not a homogeneous system, but varied from town to town, and was less comprehensive and thorough than historians make out.

The distinction between 'capitulated' and 'conquered' is a legal fiction. Within a few years of the conquest the Muslims treated the subject peoples much as they chose.

The original tribute was that paid to the preceding government; it may have been about two dinars a head in the west.

The graded poll-tax was first levied in Mesopotamia.

At first monks did not pay poll-tax.

The subject peoples at first bore the whole weight of taxation; though it is not possible to decide how heavy that was. It certainly grew heavier, but then the *dhimmis* did not bear the whole weight, for the Muslims paid land tax, the religious taxes were paid into the treasury, and Muslims and *dhimmis* alike were liable to the other burdens.

LATER DEVELOPMENTS

The poll-tax became known later as *jawāli*. When Saladin conquered Jerusalem, in 583, the Christians native to the town obtained permission to reside there by paying the poll-tax.[1] In the middle of the third century, the poll-tax from Baghdad is given as 120,000 dirhams, and again as 200,000.[2] That of Misr (Egypt, or Cairo) was 130,000 dinars in 587 and 11,400 in 816.[3] It was

---

[1] Ath., y. 583.   [2] Khurdadbeh, 125, 251.   [3] M., 1, 107.

paid according to the lunar year.[1] In 682 it was paid in Muharram, having been postponed from Ramadan, the usual date.[2]

In 674 part of Nubia was conquered, and the inhabitants given the choice between the poll-tax and death. They agreed to pay one dinar for all adult males.[3] Kalkashandi says that the poll-tax used to be in three grades—4⅙ dinars, 2$\frac{1}{12}$, and 1$\frac{39}{48}$, with 2¼ dirhams added to pay the accountant and his assistants. In the writer's own day it had grown less; the highest grade was 25 dirhams and the lowest 10.[4]

The poll-tax was paid separately before the land tax and after the dues named *hilāli*, rents of buildings, fishing dues, etc., which were paid monthly. It was paid annually, though it had been proposed to have it paid monthly for convenience in the case of a man dying or turning Muslim.[5] Lawyers differed as to what should be done when a *dhimmi* died before he had paid his tax. Some held that the payment lapsed, others that it was to be recovered from his estate.[6] There was the same difference about a convert. 'Umar II ruled that the tax ought not to be taken from a *dhimmi* for the year in which he was converted.[7] It is clear that his ruling was not accepted.

In 678 Saif ud Dīn Kalāwun abolished a tax of one dinar on the *dhimmis* over and above the poll-tax which had been paid for eighteen years. It was called *mukarrar un nasāra.*[8]

[1] M., 1, 276.   [2] Q., 3, 39.   [3] Q., 2, 130.   [4] Subh., 3, 462.
[5] M., 1, 107.   [6] Mizan, 2, 161.   [7] Ibn Sa'd, 5, 262.
[8] M., 1, 106; Q., 3, 3.

Figures giving the totals for tribute are irritating in their fewness and vagueness.

Alexandria began by paying 18,000 dinars, and in the reign of Hishām it paid 36,000. The prefect Menas exhorted 32,056 pieces of gold—presumably dinars—from the town. He was dismissed, and his successor demanded only 22,000, the rightful sum.[1] The figure 600,000 dinars, reached by assuming a population of 300,000 paying 2 dinars a head, is obviously a fiction.

A number of totals are given for Egypt as a whole.

Date A.H.
19–25. 2,000,000 dinars. 'Amr, governor.
26–35. 4,000,000   ,,   'Abdulla b. Sa'd, governor.
47–62. Surplus sent to Damascus, 600,000. Maslama, governor.
c. 107. 4,000,000. 'Abdulla b. Habhāb, finance minister.
        Expenses 2,700,783. (Tribute 2,723,783. Ibn Khurdādhbeh.)
200. 4,275,000 (2 dinars on the feddān). Māmūn, caliph.
254. The tribute had sunk to 1,800,000 (the text has 800,000,000), but Ahmad b. Tūlūn raised it to 4,000,000.
358. 3,400,000. Jawhar. (3,200,000. Ibn Hawkal.)
463. 2,800,000.[2]

These figures are enough to show that the twelve millions attributed to 'Amr and Usāma, and the fourteen millions given to 'Abdulla b. Sa'd, are exaggerated.

Three figures are given for Hims—340,000, 218,000, and 118,000 dinars. No argument can be based on them.[3] At the time of the conquest Barka

[1] B., 223 ; J.N., 384. [2] M., 1, 79, 98 ; B., 216 ; Khurdadbeh, 83 ; I.H., 108.
[3] Khurdadbeh, 76, 246, 251.

paid 13,000 dinars.[1] Ibn Khaldūn's tribute list gives it 1,000,000.

Thus the tribute in Egypt grew smaller while the rate of land tax rose from one dinar the *feddān* to seven.

Occasional acts of grace on the part of the ruler are recorded. Thus Māmūn was kind to the people of Edessa, and ordered all burdens and taxes to be removed from them. As it stands this must be an exaggeration; it may have been a temporary measure. He entered the great church and wondered at its beauty. He asked the metropolitan what its revenue was. The bishop said, ' By thy grace, O king, its wealth is great; but also much of the income is spent in the burden of the taxes laid upon it.' Māmūn then ordered that no tax should be levied on the inns, shops, baths, and mills (belonging to it), but only on gardens and agricultural land; for he said that it was not right that anything with a roof should pay taxes.[2] This idea was not peculiar to Māmūn, for two legal opinions have been preserved; that if a Muslim or a *dhimmi* builds a shop on *kharāj* land, it pays no taxes, and if Muslims settle on ownerless land and make a market, there is no tax on it.[3]

The Muslim year was lunar, so there were more calendar years than agricultural. Khālid ul Kasri stopped the intercalation in the Persian calendar. It has been noted already that the taxes of the solar year 88 were paid in 91. Apparently there was no systematic equalization of the two calendars, but from time to time a year was dropped. So in the

[1] Hakam, 170.   [2] S.A., 2, 23.   [3] B., 448.

time of Mutawakkil 241 was counted as 242 for the purpose of finance. A year was dropped at 278, at 499 two were dropped, another at 507, and two more at 565.

In the course of his reign Mu'tadid shifted Nawrūz from 11 Safar to 13 Rabī' II, which was 11 Hazīrān.[1]

MODE OF PAYING THE POLL-TAX

In a guide to the duties of a civil servant, the following instructions for the collection of poll-tax are given. It is to be collected without violence or flogging. The *dhimmi* need not sell his cattle, asses, or sheep to pay it. He has to stand while paying, and the officer who receives it sits. The *dhimmi* has to be made to feel that he is an inferior person when he pays, he is not to be treated with honour.[2]

Further details are given in this quotation. ' The *dhimmi*, Christian or Jew, goes on a fixed day in person (at first a substitute was forbidden) to the emir appointed to receive the poll-tax. He sits on a high throne. The *dhimmi* appears before him, offering the poll-tax on his open palm. The emir takes it so that his hand is on top and the *dhimmi*'s below. Then the emir gives him a blow on the neck, and one who stands before the emir drives him roughly away. . . . The public is admitted to see this show.'[3]

I have not been able to discover what authority the writer had for these statements.

In the beginning payment in kind was allowed. It is said that 'Ali accepted ropes and needles.

---

[1] M., 1, 274–81.   [2] Suli, 215.   [3] Rainer, 672.

Carcases, wine, and pigs were not accepted, but the taxpayer might sell them and pay the proceeds into the treasury.[1]

PRESENTS

The custom of allowing the governors to receive presents on festivals, particularly Nawrūz, was especially open to abuse. Probably it always existed but Arab historians have discovered the originator of it. Either Walīd b. 'Ukba or Hajjāj began it. 'Umar II stopped it, but it began afresh in the days of Māmūn, when Ahmad b. Yūsuf gave him a sack of gold.[2] During the reign of Mu'āwia, the revenue of Kūfa was fifty million dirhams and as much again in presents. Under Ibn Zubair the revenue was sixty million dirhams, and gifts amounted to twenty millions.[3]

---

[1] Kh., 69 ; Suli, 215.   [2] Suli, 220 ; Subh., 2, 409.   [3] Suli, 219.

CONCLUSION

THIS study of the relations between the government and its subjects who did not profess Islam can only produce confusion in the mind. At one moment the *dhimmi* appears as a persecuted worm who is entirely negligible, and the next complaint is made of his pernicious influence on the Muslims round him. Laws were made, observed for a time, and then forgotten till something brought them to the remembrance of the authorities. There is no constitutional growth; events move in irregular curves, not in a straight line. One feels that if events had been governed by logic, Islam would have swallowed up the subject religions; but they survive, vigorous though battered.

A few dates are fixed and some periods can be marked off roughly, though the boundaries are vague. Under the first Umayyads, the conquerors were on fairly good terms with the vanquished. Most of the minor officials were not Muslims, and many of the victors were better Arabs than Muslims. Historians delight to picture the justice of the conquerors. Take such a scene as this. 'Amr b. 1 'As was sitting on the ground in his palace with his Arabs, when the Makaukas came to visit him. A golden throne was carried with him, that he might sit on it after the manner of kings. He did so sit on it in the presence of 'Amr, who made no objection to his doing so. Thus the Muslims kept the treaty they had made with him.[1] There was, how-

[1] I. Khald., 260.

ever, a darker side to the picture. 'Amr was told
that a man in Upper Egypt, whose name was Peter,
had a treasure. As the man denied all knowledge
of any treasure, he was put in prison. 'Amr asked if
he were ever heard to enquire about any special person, and was told that he had asked after a certain
monk. 'Amr wrote to the monk, sealing the letter
with Peter's seal, ' Send me that you have.' The
messenger brought back a Syrian pot sealed with
lead; inside was a paper with the words, ' Your
money is under the big pool '. 'Amr drained the
pool, removed the flooring, and found there fifty-two
ardebbs of gold in coin. 'Amr had Peter executed
at the door of the mosque, and then all the Copts
brought out their treasures in fear of a like fate.[1]
John of Nikiou says that 'Amr was of savage
extraction, treated the Egyptians without pity, and
did not keep the treaties he had made with them.[2]

The rule of Islam was often burdensome, the
revolts in Egypt prove it. 'Umar II might order a
governor to distribute the surplus cash in his
treasury among the *dhimmis* after the needs of the
Muslims had been satisfied,[3] but as a rule they had
to provide the money which the state wanted and
got nothing for it. Probably, at first, the subjects did
not pay heavier taxes than they had paid to the
previous governments, but in one way and another
the burden grew steadily heavier. There can be no
doubt that, at the end of the first century, the reign
of 'Umar II saw the beginning of definite disabilities
for the *dhimmis*. Restrictions were placed on their
dress, and the attempt to oust them from official

---

[1] M., 1, 76.   [2] J.N., 377 ; cf. 355.   [3] Umar, 67.

posts began. It may be remarked that 'Umar II is
the typical pious persecutor, scrupulously just in his
dealings with individuals while he tries to suppress
the *dhimmis* as a class.[1] Not all of his laws were
enforced; for, in the time of Māmūn, the inhabitants
of Harrān still wore the *kubā* and long hair. His
attempt to drive the *dhimmis* from government
service was even less successful.

During the second century the Muslim spirit
hardened. In the days of Hārūn Rashīd, a lawyer
could say that idolaters were entitled to the privileges of the people of the book, yet Māmūn gave
the people of Harrān the choice between Islam and
death. At the same time the laws about dress were
made more stringent, and the idea took shape that
churches might not be built.

The next fixed point is the reign of Mutawakkil.
His laws deserve the name of persecution. Yet his
zeal was strangely impersonal, for he was on the
best of terms with his Christian doctors. His were
the most severe laws that were issued against the
dhimmis; in later times it was enough to put them
in force.

It is only fair to say that the conduct of the rulers
was often better than the law demanded. Places of
worship were built in purely Arab towns; Christians, guilty of misconduct with Muslim women,
were only fined instead of being put to death;
apostasy was not always punished with death; men
of various faiths studied under Muslim masters. Jews
and Christians were always to be found in public
service, indeed they sometimes held the highest posts.

[1] Umar; Jauzi, 104.

They could amass wealth; indeed, indiscreet display of wealth and power was often the cause of the evils that befell them. On paper, many things were forbidden them; the public celebration of weddings and funerals, feasts, and church ceremonies. It was a punishable offence to tread intentionally on the skirt of a Muslim's garment, and they had to leave the centre of the road to the Muslims.[1] Kinglake tells that, in his day in Damascus, a native Christian dared not walk on the footpath. Yet, in spite of the laws, Christians jostled Muslims, were employed by them in positions of trust, and Muslims seized the Christian feasts as opportunities of merrymaking.

Mu'tasim bought the monastery at Samarra that stood where he wanted to build his palace.[2] Other caliphs destroyed churches to obtain material for their buildings, and the mob was always ready to pillage churches and monasteries. Though *dhimmis* might enjoy great prosperity, yet always they lived on sufferance, exposed to the caprices of the ruler and the passions of the mob. The episode of al Hākim must be regarded as the freak of a mad man, and not typical of Islam. But in later times the position of the *dhimmis* did change for the worse. They were much more liable to suffer from the violence of the crowd, and the popular fanaticism was accompanied by an increasing strictness among the educated. The spiritual isolation of Islam was accomplished. The world was divided into two classes, Muslims and others, and only Islam counted. There were brilliant exceptions, but the general statement is true. If a Muslim gave any

---

[1] Fath, 1, 334.   [2] Mas.T., 357.

help to the religion of a *dhimmi*, he was to be summoned thrice to repentance, and then, if obdurate, he was to be put to death.[1] Indeed, the general feeling was that the leavings of the Muslims were good enough for the *dhimmis*.

It has been proved that 'Umar I did not destroy the library at Alexandria. In addition to other reasons, one may argue that the words put into his mouth, ' If the books agree with the Koran, they are unnecessary; if they do not, they are pernicious ', reveal the mind of a later age, when Islam had become intellectually proud. Practically the same story is told of a governor of Khorāsān in the third century.

About the covenant of 'Umar, it is only needful to collect what has been said in scattered places. Reference to the covenant does not become common till quite late. In the first century it is ignored. In the second some of its provisions are sometimes observed. By 200 it existed in the traditional form, but with many minor variations. The agreements made by Muslim commanders with conquered towns are not modelled on it. Some of its provisions seem to have been first enacted by 'Umar II, which may have helped the attribution of it to his greater namesake. The covenant mentioned by Abū Yūsuf may have been an early form of this document, but probably he had in mind some special treaty or a general claim of rights made by the *dhimmis*. The covenant was drawn up in the schools of law, and came to be ascribed, like so much else, to 'Umar I.

[1] Fath, 1, 334.

ORIGINAL AUTHORITIES

A.M.	..	History, Abu l Maḥāsin Taghriberdi.
A.S.	..	Churches and Monasteries of Egypt, Abū Sāliḥ.
Abu Daud	..	Sunan, Delhi, A.H. 1318.
Abu l Fida	..	History. (References are given to the year only.)
Agh.	..	Kitāb ul Aghāni.
Amali	..	Al Amāli, Ḳāli, 1926.
'Arib.	..	Continuation of Tabari.
Ath.	..	History, Ibn ul Athīr. (References to the year only.)
Azdi	..	Futūḥ ush Shām, Al Azdi, 1854.
B.	..	Futūḥ ul Buldān, Balādhuri.
B.H.	..	Chronicle, Bar Hebræus, Paris.
B.H. Eccl.	..	Ecclesiastical Chronicle. Bar Hebræus.
B.H. Mu.	..	Mukhtaṣar ud Duwal. Bar Hebræus, 1890.
B.M.	..	Greek Papyri in the British Museum, Vol. 4.
Benj.	..	Benjamin of Tudela, ed. Gruenhut and Adler. 1903–.
Br. Ch.	..	Chronology of Ancient Nations, al Birūni.
Bukhari	..	Saḥīḥ.
Bundari	..	History of the Seljuk Turks, Bundāri.
C.M.	..	Chronica Minora, C.S.C.O., Ser. III, Vol. 4.
Ch.M.	..	Chahār Maḳāla, Niẓāmi, 1909.
Dawlatshah	..	Memoirs of the Poets.
Ecl.	..	Eclipse of the Abbasid Caliphate.
Elias	..	Elias of Nisibis, 1884.
Eut.	..	History, Eutychius.
Fath	..	Fatḥ ul 'Ali ul Mālik, A.H. 1319.
Fih.	..	Fihrist, Abu n Nadīm.
Ghazi	..	An Answer to the Dhimmis, Ghāzi b. ul Wāsiṭi, J.A.O.S., 1921.

Hakam	.. Futūḥ Miṣr, Ibn ʿAbd ul Ḥakam.
Hamdani	.. Geography of Arabia, Hamdāni.
Husn	.. Ḥuṣn ul Muhāḍara, Suyūti, A.H. 1321.
I.A.	.. History, Ibn ʿAsākir.
I.H.	.. Kitāb ul masālik walmamālik, Ibn Hawkal.
I.R.	.. Kitāb ul Aʿlāk un nafīsa, Ibn Rusteh.
I. Khald.	.. Prolegomena, Ibn Khaldūn, Beirut.
I. Khall.	.. Biographical Dictionary, Ibn Khallikān, A.H. 1299.
Ibn Saʿd	.. Kitāb ut ṭabaḳāt ul kabīr, Ibn Saʿd.
Ihya	.. Iḥyā ʿulūm ud dīn, Ghazāli, A.H. 1312.
Ikd	.. Al ʿIḳd ul farīd, Ibn ʿabd rabbihi.
Iyas	.. History, Ibn Iyās, A.H. 1311.
J.N.	.. John of Nikiou, Journal Asiatique, 1879.
Jahiz B.	.. Kitāb ul bayān, Al Jāḥiẓ, A.H. 1313.
Jahiz H.	.. Kitāb ul ḥayawān, Al Jāḥiẓ, A.H. 1323.
Joshua	.. Joshua Stylites, ed. Wright.
K.	.. Book of Governors and Judges, Kindi.
Kh.	.. Kitāb ul kharāj, Abū Yūsuf Yaʿḳūb, A.H. 1332.
Khurdadbeh	.. Kitāb ul mamālik walmasālik, Ibn Khurdādhbeh.
Kifti	.. Tarīkh ul Ḥukamā, al Kifti.
L.A.	.. Lisān ul ʿarab.
Lang.	.. Michel le Syrien, trans. Langlois.
M.	.. Khiṭaṭ, Maḳrīzi, A.H. 1270.
Mak.	.. Nafḥ uṭ ṭīb, Makkari.
Mas.	.. Murūj udh dhahab, Masʿūdi.
Mas.T.	.. Kitāb ut tanbīh wal ishrāf, Masʿūdi.
Mizan	.. Kitāb ul mīzān, Ash Shaʿrāni, A.H. 1306.
Mubarrad	.. Kāmil, Mubarrad.
Mud.	.. Al mudawwana ul kubra, A.H. 1324.
Muk.	.. Geography, Mukaddisi.
Must.	.. Mustaṭraf, Egypt, A.H. 1306.
Muwashshah	.. Al Marzubāni, Egypt, A.H. 1343.
Nish.	.. Nishwār ul Muḥāḍara.
P.S.R.	.. Papyri Schott Reinhardt.
Q.	.. Histoire des Sultanes Mamlukes, trans. Quatremere.

Rahmat	..	Rahmat ul Umma (on the margin of Mizan).
Rainer	..	Fuehrer durch die Ausstellung Erzherzog Rainer.
Raudatain	..	Kitāb ur raudatain fi akhbār id daulatain, A.H. 1287.
S.	..	History of the Patriarchs, Severus, ed. Seybold.
S.A.	..	Anonymous Syriac Chronicle, C.S.C.O., Ser. III, Vols. 14, 15.
Sefernameh	..	Paris, 1881.
Siyasetnameh	..	Paris, 1891.
Subh.	..	Subḥ ul a'sha, Ḳalḳashandi.
Suli	..	Adab ul kuttāb, A's Sūli, A.H. 1341.
T.	..	Annals, Ṭabari.
Tabak.	..	Ṭabaḳāt ul aṭibbā, Ibn abī Usaibī'a.
Thomas	..	Book of Governors, Thomas of Marga.
Umar	..	Life of 'Umar II, 'Abdulla b. 'Abd ul Ḥakam, 1927.
Umar Jawzi	..	Life by 'Abd ur Rahmān ul Jawzi.
Umda	..	Al 'Umda, Ibn Rashīḳ, 1907.
Umm	..	Kitāb ul Umm, Shāfe'i.
Uyun	..	'Uyūn ul akhbār, Ibn Ḳutaiba, Egypt, 1925.
Viziers	..	Kitāb ul wuzarā, ed. Amedroz.
Y.	..	Geographical Dictionary, Yākūt. (References are not given when the names of places stand in alphabetical order.)
Y.Ir.	..	Biographical Dictionary.
Yahya	..	Kitāb ul Kharāj, Yaḥya.
Yak.	..	History, Ya'ḳubi.
Yak.B.	..	Kitāb ul Buldān, Ya'ḳūbi.

MODERN BOOKS

Andrae	..	Die Person Muhammads.
Barthold	..	Turkestan down to the Mongol Invasion.
Browne	..	Year among the Persians (First Edition).

Caetani	..	Annali dell' Islam.
Cheikho	..	Le Christianisme en Arabie avant l' Islam (Arabic).
Gottheil	..	Dhimmis and Muslims in Egypt (Old Testament and Semitic Studies in memory of W. R. Harper).
Juynboll	..	Handbuch des islamischen Gesetzes.
Mez	..	Die Renaissance des Islams.
Rylands	..	Bulletin of the John Rylands Library.

INDEX